"All of us want to improve  no shortage of answers a embarked on a journey t wanting. But in the process, she learned about herself, and more importantly about her relationship with her Savior. This book is the fruit of that journey, and it's one that will serve anyone who has believed that self-help books and tactics are the answer to their needs. Giles has been in your shoes, and she is a friend who invites you back to God's purposes for you."

**COURTNEY REISSIG,** Author, *Teach Me to Feel: Worshiping Through the Psalms in Every Season of Life*

"With precision and skill, Tieler Giles identifies why self-help promises much but delivers little, and points us instead to the person of Christ in whom all things are done, not to-do. I appreciated her wealth of experience as a life coach; the acknowledgement of where self-help can have value; her honesty and her witty observations. This book is joyful, real, comprehensive and practical. Don't just put it on your to-do list—read it!"

**LINDA ALLCOCK,** Author, *Deeper Still: Finding Clear Minds and Full Hearts through Biblical Meditation;* Staff Member, The Globe Church, London, UK

"Truth and grace mark the ministry of our Lord, and they also mark Tieler's perceptive book on ditching the endlessly exhausting pursuit of self-help. Full of insight into the human heart, *How to Ditch the How-to* will expose your need—and Christ's perfect, abundant grace."

**KRISTEN WETHERELL,** Author, *Help for the Hungry Soul* and *Hope When It Hurts*

"This book offers nothing short of grace to the strive-weary among us. In its pages, Tieler Giles helps us all ease off our own go-go-go agendas and offers a road toward living as God intended."

**CARYN RIVADENEIRA,** Author, *Saints of Feather and Fang*

"So many of us are seeking inner healing and transformation. Yet, there comes a point when we desperately need more than the latest trendy tools or tried-and-true religious rituals. In *How to Ditch the How-to,* Tieler Giles shows us how we change and grow best: as we experience a sincere, deep relationship with the greatest Helper."

**LAKESHIA POOLE,** Author, *Faith Beats Fear*

"Take it from someone who's been there: Tieler Giles really has put all the latest self-help trends to the test (manifesting, meditating, setting intentions, positive self-talk—you name it, she's done it!). In *How to Ditch the How-to,* Tieler takes us with her on her years of trying to find happiness and fulfillment within herself. She shares candidly the effort and exhaustion, the high hopes and deep disillusionment. And then she shares with us the relief, peace, and soul-deep joy she finally found in Jesus. No doubt every reader will see some of herself in Tieler's story. Who among us hasn't succumbed to self-help? But Tieler tells us the better and truer story of who we are, in light of who our Creator is and how he made us to find abundant life in him. Tieler's story is authentic, transparent, and ultimately full of the best news there is. If you're tired of trying to keep up, then take up this book and find real rest."

**JEN OSHMAN,** Author, *Enough About Me*
and *Cultural Counterfeits*

# TIELER GILES

# How to Ditch the How-to

## Embracing Grace in Place of Self-Improvement

thegoodbook
COMPANY

How to Ditch the How-To
© Tieler Giles, 2024

Published by:
The Good Book Company

thegoodbook.com | thegoodbook.co.uk
thegoodbook.com.au | thegoodbook.co.nz | thegoodbook.co.in

Cover design by Faceout Studio | Design and art direction by André Parker

ISBN: 9781802541304 | JOB-007937 | Printed in India

*To all those searching for more*

# CONTENTS

# INTRODUCTION

"**W**hen will it be enough?"

That was the question that brought to an end a four-year journey to find myself, fix myself, and live my best life. I was living in Brooklyn, New York. Spring had sprung, and my discontentment was as pervasive as the pollen. Here I was yet again, scrutinizing other people's lives, wondering where I went wrong and what I needed to do differently to make life work.

I knew there was more to life than what I was experiencing.

"I just need to refocus and recalibrate," I thought as my feet hit the floor.

But that morning, I could not summon my "higher self," nor could I create another personal development plan: *journal more, read more, run more, cook more; be more grateful, mindful, positive, and open.*

I wanted none of it. I was done. I had spent years up to my eyeballs in self-help strategies, methods, and tools, hoping to reach my "fullest potential." My vision? That wondrous day when I would stop chasing change, finally content with myself and my life. Yet all my striving and searching had not brought more satisfaction but less.

Maybe you're in a similar place. You've been working hard but don't feel any closer to the life you imagined. Maybe you feel stuck and unsure of what to do at this point. You wonder if life is *this* hard for other people. Or perhaps life is improving, and you want to make sure change sticks this time. You want to finally get over the hump to stay motivated and consistent. You understand real change takes time, but you're willing to do what it takes.

Lying in bed that morning, I could no longer ignore the longing in my heart for something more. I had come to the end of the road—and to the end of myself.

Then I heard an unmistakable answer.

*"When will it be enough?"*

*"It won't."*

I would never find "enough" by doing more of the same thing. There was something bigger, *someone* bigger, whose help I needed.

Whether we identify as a Christian or not, I think we all get to points in our lives when we feel outmatched. Wherever you are spiritually—if you're walking with Jesus, have wandered away, or find faith to be altogether complicated—this book is for you.

*How to Ditch the How-To* is about letting go of self-help and receiving God's grace to live life well. You won't find strategies or tips to believe in yourself more, love yourself more, or overcome your limitations. Instead, I want to point you to the one whose grace is more than enough. I believe the good news that Jesus shared some 2,000 years ago is the answer to what we've been searching for.

Part 1 of this book examines our striving to change. We'll unpack the real problem at hand, God's plan, and our dilemma. Part 2 delves into the pursuit of happiness, love, and everything in between. I share some self-help stories (brace yourself), and we'll uncover what the Bible has to say. Part 3 explores what awaits on the other side of striving and what we stand to gain when we let go.

Along the way, we'll consider what self-help advice you might have come across on the subject before comparing it with what God has to say on the matter in the Bible. I believe the word of God not only inspires, but it also has the power to transform. Given that, you will also find at the end of each chapter one key takeaway to help you embrace grace and a Bible verse for reflection.

When Jesus preached what's known as his "Sermon on the Mount," he invited those gathered that day into a new way of living. Many of them were struggling and tired, and in desperate need of hope and healing. Notably, Jesus did not call for them to fix themselves or save themselves but instead to turn from themselves and turn to God. That same invitation is available to you and me today.

As you journey through this book, I pray that the pressure to work harder and achieve more will subside—that you will shift from feeling discouraged and unsatisfied to experiencing gratitude and joy. I believe that you really *can* have peace, wholeness, and fulfillment on the inside—well before one single thing changes on the outside. Yes, the path to change is challenging. But you don't have to walk it alone.

Together, let's explore how to ditch the how-to and embrace grace in place of self-improvement.

# PART ONE

# CHAPTER 1

# THE CHANGE

*"Nothing changes if nothing changes."*

**Anonymous**

I read my very first self-help book when I was eleven or twelve: *Chicken Soup for the Soul.* I assume now it must have belonged to my mother, although when I found it, it had yet to be opened. First published in 1993, this popular book—and eventual series—featured a collection of inspirational true stories that taught life principles that readers could apply to their own lives.

There I was, a middle-school student—dealing with cliques, crushes, and mood swings—reading stories about empty-nesters, guardian angels, and cats who rescued their owners. On the surface, I couldn't relate to any of it.

Yet these stories, in some strange and magical way, put my pre-teen troubles in perspective, offering courage and hope. If Susan could find happiness after a heartbreaking divorce, I thought to myself, surely I could survive a friend being upset with me because her boyfriend told his friend who told our other friend that he had a crush on me. (I think that's how that went.)

For the first time, I realized I had a say in what I thought and how I felt. In other words, I could change.

## READY FOR CHANGE

We all want change, one way or another. Whether it's a more fulfilling career, greater financial stability, healing from past trauma, or better gut health—our desire for change is a natural response to areas of our lives that aren't working well. And that desire is not a bad thing. In fact, that impulse and ability to exercise agency over ourselves and our environment is part of what makes us human. So, if you've picked up this book in hopes of change, you're in good company.

The billion-dollar question, though, is *how?* I mean that literally. From books to programs to workshops to conferences, there is a multi-billion-dollar industry ready to help us help ourselves. The hope of change is the promise that lies behind every self-help strategy. Indeed, there is no shortage of principles and advice to learn, grow, and live life well.

Yet change is hard. Maybe, like me, you've discovered that already. We want to wake up an hour earlier, but instead we stay up an hour later. We want to be kinder, but instead we criticize others. We want to save money, but instead we buy things we don't really need.

We convince ourselves that the next time will be different, if only we try a little harder. So we give it another go, employing a new method or technique to change our lives and ourselves for the better.

But real change isn't just about changing behavior.

Willpower will only get us so far. If we want change to last, we need to go beneath the surface. That's why some self-help experts focus on what's called "mindset"—your mental attitude. Our mindset determines things like how we view challenges, rebound from setbacks, and respond to feedback. The key thing about mindset is that it's something we can learn, and therefore it can be improved—and sometimes the results are impressive.

When most people set out to change their lives, they tend to focus on the tangible, external goal: save more money, for example. A better alternative, according to scholars, is to focus on the attitudes and beliefs that will help you reach your goal. Whether it's letting go of comparison, embracing contentment, or celebrating small wins, these are all mental habits that can be built—and that in the long term will help you save money.

I don't know what changes you're looking to make in your life. But I do know that all the mindset champions are onto something. Indeed, we find a similar idea in the Bible. One of its writers, the apostle Paul, said this to a group of Christians he was concerned about: "Do not conform to the pattern of this world, but be transformed by the renewing of your mind. Then you will be able to test and approve what God's will is—his good, pleasing and perfect will" (Romans 12:2). You see, our mindset can be a help or a hindrance to living the life God desires for us—a life that is "good," in the fullest sense of the word.

If we want change, instead of focusing solely on the outer world, we need to start paying attention to our inner world. What is happening on the outside of us is often connected to what is happening on the inside.

If we desire outward change, we must focus on our inward being.

## CHANGE THROUGH INNER WORK

For nearly a decade, television viewers across America tuned in to watch dysfunctional families deal with serious and oftentimes outrageous personal challenges in *Iyanla, Fix My Life*. This self-help television show began in 2012, and featured life coach and relationship expert Iyanla Vanzant helping people take the first steps on their road to recovery.

I wasn't a loyal viewer, but the show and its charismatic star are etched in my memory. No matter what the location, family, or issue at hand were, at some point during each episode, Vanzant would proudly proclaim her signature line: that the person wanting change needed to "do the work!"

A mom dealing with freeloading adult children needed to "do the work" to release the guilt she felt from her divorce and heal the pain of a broken relationship with her father. A guy with anger issues (and holes in his walls) needed to "do the work" to confront the low expectations his family had of him and to adopt new beliefs.

Many self-help authors explore this internal work, offering strategies to improve our inner world—what's sometimes called "soul work."

So then, what is the soul? While definitions vary, it's perhaps best to understand our soul as the internal, non-material part of who we are. Think of the soul as your complete inner self: your mind, will, and emotions. It is your soul that gives life to your body and reflects things like your personality, passions, and preferences. When you encounter an obstacle during the day, it is in your soul that you think, feel, and decide to respond. Therefore, the condition of your soul influences your way of life and the quality of your life.

Self-help strategies abound on how we care for the soul. One popular idea is that we need to connect with our true or authentic self. According to Martha Beck, a sociologist and life coach to media megastar Oprah Winfrey, we live in a culture that tells us what to think and how to live. When we follow these rules, we distance ourselves from our essential being.

The work then is about uncovering our soul or, as Beck puts it, "finding your own north star."[1] In her book of the same name, she encourages readers to make choices based on their instincts rather than what they've been told or made to believe.

In one sense, Beck has a similar warning to the one we read from the Bible earlier; we cannot let the world determine who we are, nor does the world know what's best for us. If we want to be free from the illusions and pressure of the outside world, we need to address our souls.

The trouble is that inner work isn't always easy work. Exploring the past, uncovering false beliefs, and nursing emotional wounds is no walk in the park. Renowned psychiatrist Carl Jung once said, "People will do anything, no matter how absurd, in order to avoid facing their own souls."[2]

But I suspect, if you've picked up this book, that you are ready to get real and are ready for real change. Yes, that may feel uncomfortable at times. There will likely be some unexpected twists and turns. But that's what life is about, right?

So, given that, here's a tough truth to consider.

Our souls are kind of a mess. They are all over the place. One minute we're chill, the next minute we're looking for a fight. We think one way and feel another. We say one thing and do another. We do the things we don't want to do, and we don't do the things we want to do. If we heed Beck's advice to follow our instincts, we won't be going in one direction for very long.

But there is hope. The Bible tells us that we find rest for our souls in God (Psalm 62:1). God has the power to renew our minds, heal our hearts, and restore our souls.

That's the headline. Yet there's more of the story to uncover. We've gone deep in this chapter. But we haven't yet gone deep enough. You see, we all have habits, dispositions, and behaviors that we want to change. However, they are not the problem but a symptom. Addressing symptoms provides temporary relief. Ibuprofen helps with pain—but it will not repair damaged tissue or address tooth decay. Real change requires us to get to the root.

The root of our problem is much bigger than us. But thankfully, so is the solution.

## EMBRACING GRACE

God has the power to renew our minds, heal our hearts, and restore our souls.

## MEMORY VERSE

*Do not conform to the pattern of this world, but be transformed by the renewing of your mind. Then you will be able to test and approve what God's will is—his good, pleasing and perfect will. (Romans 12:2)*

CHAPTER 2

# THE PROBLEM

*"A problem well put is half-solved."*[3]

**John Dewey**

I mbolo Mbue's debut novel, *Behold the Dreamers*, details the experiences of two New York City families during the 2008 financial crisis: Neni and Jende Jonga, African immigrants who leave Cameroon to fulfill the American dream, and Clark and Cindy Edwards, a wealthy, white family who appear to be living the dream. The book examines a number of critical themes, including what it means, and what it takes, to succeed, the impact of race and class on upward mobility, and the universal pursuit of happiness.

The Jongas and the Edwardses live in two very different worlds yet share the same desire to better themselves and their lives. I'm guessing that's true for most people reading this too. Maybe, like the Jongas, you've beaten the odds to accomplish more than most thought possible. You have a big vision for the future but see so many obstacles standing in the way. Or perhaps, like Clark and Cindy, you've achieved what most would call success but don't feel quite satisfied or content.

The unrelenting quest for a better life seems to be as natural to us as breathing. There is, deep inside each of us, a hunger for something more and better. But where are we trying to go? Who are we hoping to become? What is that better reality out there, beyond more things and nicer stuff?

These were the questions I asked clients as I trained to become a life coach many years ago. They were the same questions I had been wrestling with for years myself, poring over self-help book after self-help book, article after article. I realize now that, while I was asking the right questions, I was looking in the wrong place for answers.

There is a reason why your heart longs for more— why you question if you're good enough and fear at times that you may not be. We all have problems on our hands, for sure. Yet, they are not the *real* problem. There is a fundamental problem—the root of all problems in fact.

The struggles we face in this world, inwardly and outwardly, find their origin in a teeny, tiny word but a really big problem: *sin*. What we are experiencing are the effects of sin and our resulting separation from God.

I know, talking about sin is very unpopular and kind of a downer. It brings up all sorts of unfun ideas like judgment and punishment and long lists of do's and do not's. But allow me to share another point of view: sin is not primarily a behavioral issue but a relational one. When God created humanity, his intention was for us to live in close relationship with him. We were created to honor God, choose his ways, and take pleasure in the good things he created.

But instead of trusting in and submitting to God, we choose to go our own way and decide for ourselves what is best. We live in a world that is doing its own thing and is suffering the consequences. A world that worships some people and discards others. A world where we struggle with contentment, resent our friends, don't keep our word, and feel bad about all of it.

Here's what I want you to know: it's not just you. If life is not how you would like it, it's not because you've drawn some cosmic short straw. Something *is* the matter, but it's not *just* your problem; it's a universal condition.

Let's unpack how we got here and what's really going on. We're going to the first book of the Bible, Genesis, which tells the story of where we came from. If you're new to the Bible, you'll find that there are some unusual things going on in this story—things that seem improbable to the natural mind. Yet the supernatural is just that: existing outside what is normal. To believe in God at all calls that we be open and curious—and that's what I encourage you to be as we enter the story.

## IN THE BEGINNING

It was the perfect set-up. God created the universe, and everything in creation had its place and purpose. God provided a beautiful garden as a home for his people. And there was a closeness and intimacy between God and humanity. In fact, there was peace and harmony among every living thing. It was paradise. There were no rules and no need for them—except one:

> And the LORD God commanded the man, "You are free
> to eat from any tree in the garden; but you must not
> eat from the tree of the knowledge of good and evil, for
> when you eat from it you will certainly die."
>
> *(Genesis 2:16-17)*

After God gave the man, Adam, this command, he went on to create a woman, Eve: the mother of all human beings.

Fast forward to one fateful day in the garden. Eve is out and about, enjoying the splendor of God's creation when Satan comes to her in the form of a serpent. He asks Eve if God *really* said what he said. His primary intention is to get Eve to question the truthfulness and goodness of God. When Eve replies that God told them not to eat from the tree of knowledge or they will die, the serpent says that God is lying:

> "You will not certainly die," the serpent said to the
> woman. "For God knows that when you eat from it
> your eyes will be opened, and you will be like God,
> knowing good and evil." (3:4-5)

This tree, at the center of it all, was far more than a food source. It represented a choice to believe what God had said or believe the enemy's lie—to believe that God wanted the best for them or to believe that God could not be trusted. Despite all the evidence to the contrary, God's children bought the lie—hook, line, and sinker. Both Adam and Eve ate the fruit, and everything changed.

Their disobedience was met with God's just anger. His word proved true: life in every sense of the word was lost. Spiritual death—separation of the soul from

God—happened immediately. The man and woman could no longer live in the garden with God; and once evicted, they also lost access to the tree of life (v 22). With that, physical death—separation of the soul from the body—became inevitable. Adam and Eve would get old, get sick, and eventually die.

Believing a lie drove a wedge between humanity and God—since a relationship of love can only be built on truth. The man and woman were given the power to choose, and they chose to disobey God. They rejected what he had provided in search of something better. Instead of trusting him, they chose self-sufficiency and self-reliance. The concern of their hearts became then—and is ours today—having, doing, and being enough. Yet the burden to control, fix, and figure out life is more than we have been designed to bear.

## CONFRONTING FALSE BELIEFS

What we believe is important. If our thoughts can cause us to have a bad day, our beliefs have the power to determine our very existence. Our beliefs and thoughts are connected: what we think consistently over time becomes a belief. The field of psychology explores false beliefs in great detail—and with good reason. A false belief is just as powerful as a belief that is true.

Psychologists believe we form false or limiting beliefs as a defense mechanism to protect ourselves from emotional and psychological pain. Believing you have to be perfect, for example, prevents you from taking a chance and possibly failing. While false beliefs can make us feel better, they can also hold us hostage and keep us stuck.

The story from Genesis that we just unpacked shows us that, in one sense, all of our problems originate from false beliefs. Just as it was with Adam and Eve, so too with us: God speaks the truth, but instead we believe lies. This is a problem for all sorts of reasons: it puts us on a collision course with God's justice; it leads us to hurt other people who are precious to him; and it also causes a restless dissatisfaction in our internal world—the very thing that drives us to self-help for answers.

So how do we discern the truth from error? In a world where everyone claims to know the truth—or that truth doesn't exist at all—it can be difficult to know what to believe. False beliefs don't always sound like lies, especially if you grow up believing them or if they are prevalent in the culture. But the good news is that God has spoken to us clearly in his word, the Bible. Therefore, it's critically important that we face our assumptions, and our souls, and "do the work" of discovering where our beliefs run counter to the truth as God has revealed it.

Let's examine four major areas of belief to uncover the lies that may be causing challenges in your inner and outer worlds. We're only going to scratch the surface here—later in the book, we'll return to many of these themes. But for now, consider which, if any, you find yourself questioning.

## 1. WHAT YOU BELIEVE ABOUT GOD

Growing up, I believed God was a gigantic being in the sky who'd "got the whole world in his hands," as the song goes. He was strong and powerful, but he seemed far away. As I got older, I questioned how interested

God really was in what I was doing or how I was doing. Surely he had far greater matters to attend to than my final exams or dating life. He just seemed too big for the small things in life.

When we believe God isn't present or engaged, we tend to take matters into our own hands. We may stay up all night, anxious and stressed, trying to figure things out. If we believe God is impersonal or indifferent, we may have a hard time going to him for what we need or trusting that he will take care of us.

Or perhaps we believe the lie of the serpent in the garden: that God doesn't have our best interests at heart. We believe that he's withholding something good from us. If we believe that, then, like Adam and Eve, we'll end up doing our own thing, believing it will lead to joy—only for it to create an even bigger mess.

Here's the truth: God is near and available to all who seek him. The Bible tells us that he is an "ever-present help in trouble" to those who trust in him (Psalm 46:1). He loves you more than you can imagine, and all his words to you are for your good (Proverbs 30:5).

## 2. WHAT YOU BELIEVE ABOUT YOURSELF

We live in a world that tells us to be ourselves... just better. There's always a little bit more—or a lot more—for us to do and have. The entire advertising industry is built on this belief! The message is loud and clear: *You aren't doing enough and you don't have enough.* What makes this belief so powerful is another fundamental belief: that our worth as human beings is connected to how well do and how much we have. No wonder so many of us are overextended and exhausted.

Another lie that has our tanks to almost empty is that we can't be weak or fail. You may feel the stakes are too high. There seems to be so much riding on what you're able to achieve. Or it can feel like you're the only one who can handle the situation.

The truth is that our worth is not based on what we do but in who we are: precious human beings, created "in the image of God," to reflect his goodness (Genesis 1:27).

At the same time, part of being human is being finite. Our natural limits are not a bad thing. In fact, God's power can be shown most strongly when we are weak (2 Corinthians 12:9). The Bible also tells us that sin causes our souls to be unwell—but when we recognize that and go to the one who can help, we can find true healing (Luke 5:31-32).

### 3. WHAT YOU BELIEVE ABOUT PEOPLE

If there's one thing that can create anxiety in our souls, it is the thoughts and opinions of others—whether they are friends or colleagues, or perhaps a particularly significant person in our family. Underneath these feelings is a belief that, ultimately, it's these people who determine who we are and how life will go. We believe that people have the power to make or break us.

As a result, we may work really hard to gain their approval. We may exaggerate our accomplishments or dim our light. We may hide our true feelings or use flattery to sooth theirs. We might even consider this to be love. But when we believe people hold our lives in their hands, we are motivated not by love but by fear; we're ultimately acting for our own sake, not theirs.

Or maybe we swing to the other extreme: striving to "be more selfish," looking after ourselves, and cutting out friends and family who don't make us feel good.

The Bible's very first story shows us that God created us as relational beings (Genesis 2:18-23). Relationships *are* important. But they're designed to exist in the context of a relationship with him. God has the ultimate and final say on who we are. He defines us, provides for us, and gives us life: physically and spiritually. "Fear of man will prove to be a snare, but whoever trusts in the LORD is kept safe" (Proverbs 29:25).

## 4. WHAT YOU BELIEVE ABOUT LIFE

From the very beginning, humankind has been searching for the secret to life. We want to know how to make sense of it—and take control of it.

Let's face it. Life can feel unfair and unpredictable—random, even. Given that, we hoard toilet tissue and refuse to let people over in traffic. We prioritize money and being liked because we think these things determine our trajectory. Whatever will tip the scales—a rabbit's foot, healing crystals, or astrology—we'll give it a try.

The creation story shows us the truth: that life is not random. God put us here on purpose and with purpose: to live as his representatives, ruling his creation and reflecting his glory (Genesis 1:26-28). And God hasn't disappeared from the scene since then. He's still the ultimate source of power and authority over everything that exists (2 Chronicles 20:6). Nothing in life is without purpose or outside his control.

## BEYOND SELF-HELP: RESTORATION

Here's where we've gotten to: since Adam and Eve, our problems stem from false beliefs about who God is, who we are, what we're here for, and how we relate to others. God has spoken truth, but we've been sucked in by lies. Yet changing our beliefs is not as simple as reading words on a page and nodding along or even agreeing with the truth.

Countless self-help books explore false beliefs and the importance of challenging our BS: that is, our belief system. The advice is to identify the belief and then swap it out for healthier, more helpful beliefs. While many of us recognize that our beliefs hold us back, it can be difficult to shift our thinking. We work hard to disregard one false belief, only to have another spring up in its place.

For example, imagine that Tracey believes she is too old to go back to school. She recognizes her limiting belief and decides to adopt an alternative belief: that age and wisdom will benefit her greatly in her pursuits. She aligns with this new belief and moves forward. Except, months later, Tracey is now convinced that the problem is not her age but that she's not smart enough to handle the challenging coursework.

Trying to overcome false beliefs is like catching a mouse in your apartment only to see another one days later dart underneath your stove. Which is definitely one thing I do not miss about living in New York. As my building superintendent explained it, Mickey and his friends would continue to visit unless we found and filled the hole in my unit serving as their entry point. It turned out that my mouse problem was really a problem with the condition of my apartment.

The Bible's response to our problems is radically different than—and greater to—what we find in self-help. The biblical response to false beliefs is not simply to think or believe differently. God wants to do more than fix one or two wrong thoughts. He wants to restore our condition completely.

This was the message that a prophet named Ezekiel told God's people, as recorded in the Old Testament of the Bible. Ezekiel lived at a time when God's people had consistently failed to honor God. They believed the lie that worshiping other gods would bring them greater peace and prosperity; they believed the lie that dishonesty, greed, and violence didn't really matter. Generation after generation, God had sent them messengers (called prophets) to point them back to the truth. Sometimes the people listened, but it never lasted; over time, it grew worse. Eventually, as a result, they were evicted from their homeland, in the same way that Adam and Eve had been evicted from theirs.

But when all seemed lost, God sent Ezekiel with a message of hope. He said that God would do the inner work to change the condition of their souls:

> *I will give you a new heart and put a new spirit in you;*
> *I will remove from you your heart of stone and give you*
> *a heart of flesh. (Ezekiel 36:26)*

God's desire for them was that they turn from themselves and turn to him. Knowing they needed next-level help, he promised to help them from the inside out.

## IT'S TIME TO ASK FOR HELP

My oldest niece has always been the child who insists on doing things herself. One day years ago, we were playing with LEGOs together. She was around four at the time.

"Is that a house you're building?" I asked, watching her lock a few pieces together. No response. She continued to build, this time trying to add windows and a door. I could see her frustration mounting. "Can I help you?" I asked. Silence. I decided to leave her to it and got up to head to the kitchen.

I hadn't made it four steps before I heard a piercing scream. I turn around to watch her smash the house to pieces Godzilla-style and then clear her Little Tikes table in one fell swoop. Fast forward 15 minutes and two patient parents later, she came out of her room and found a seat on my lap.

"Auntie, I'm sorry for throwing my LEGOs," she said with the sweetest, most sincere look on her face. "Can you still help me?"

I replied with the biggest hug I could give her. "All you ever have to do is ask," I said.

Doing it her way did not work out so well for my niece. But she found the help she needed when she recognized that while she could not do it on her own, there was someone who loved her who could.

Perhaps you've been trying for years to build your life by yourself. It's hard work, I know. The good news is that you don't have to go it alone. To receive help, however, you'll have to stop doing it your way and instead turn to the Master Builder himself. That's what we'll consider next.

## EMBRACING GRACE

God will do the inner work to change the condition of our souls.

## MEMORY VERSE

*I will give you a new heart and put a new spirit in you; I will remove from you your heart of stone and give you a heart of flesh. (Ezekiel 36:26)*

**CHAPTER 3**

# THE PLAN

*"Grace means that all of your mistakes now serve a
purpose instead of serving shame."*

**Unknown**

It was the last Sunday in June, 2005. I had moved to
Atlanta in January of that year, fresh out of graduate
school, and began attending church with a couple of
friends. I had gone to church more in those five months
than I had in the previous five years. When I left home
for college, I didn't plan to stop going to church. I guess
I just never made plans to go either.

Growing up, I went to church every Sunday with my
family and got baptized when I was eleven years old. I
remember as a child knowing that God loved me and
experiencing his grace as I got older: quelling friendship
drama, healing loved ones, and enabling me to meet my
college sweetheart and land my first job.

As I began this new chapter in Atlanta, I knew I would
need God more than ever. It was time to get serious
about being a Christian. That meant giving God more
of my time and attention—hence church on Sundays.

Up until that point, I believed in Jesus. But I wasn't exactly sure what that meant, outside of going to heaven. What difference did following Jesus really make in my day-to-day life? After five months of faithful churchgoing, I still wasn't entirely sure. But sitting in church on that fateful June day, something stirred inside of me demanding to know more.

"If you want to give your life to Christ today, this is your invitation." It was the same altar call I had heard every Sunday. But something that day pulled at me. I could not shake the feeling that the preacher was speaking directly to me. But I wasn't ready to make any commitments. After all, I was finally going to church regularly. Wasn't that enough for now? Besides, what was I even agreeing to? What if I had a change of heart or realized the whole Jesus thing really wasn't for me?

As my thoughts began to race, I heard another voice but not my own.

"Come."

I'm not sure whether I heard it with my ears or my heart, but it was clear. Tears began to fall as I began to walk. Before I knew it, I was at the front of the church, about to embark on the journey of a lifetime.

Jesus and I had been acquainted. He was like that friend from work—you're friendly, but you're not close. You've never been over to her house, and she's never gotten an invitation to yours. You like her, but you can't really vouch for her. If you were in a jam, you would call half a dozen other people before even thinking to ring her. That was me and Jesus.

But that day, I wanted to know him personally. I wanted to know who all the talk was about. Did he alter destinies? Did he transform lives? Was he the ultimate source of truth? That's what the Bible said. But to trust in Jesus, I would have to take the next step. That day, I accepted God's offer of salvation through Jesus and committed my life to following him.

## JESUS CHRIST—A CLOSER LOOK

You would be hard pressed to find a more notable person in human history than Jesus of Nazareth. Our calendar is based on what was thought to be the year of his birth. Two of our biggest holidays, Christmas and Easter, celebrate his birth and resurrection. The Bible, which contains the story of his ministry, is the most read, most translated, and highest-selling book of all time. Not to mention that almost a third of the world's population identify as Christian.[4]

According to scholars, Jesus was about 30 years old when he began his public ministry and 33 years old at the time of his death. It's quite astonishing to consider his influence on culture and society, given such a brief period of activity. Without a doubt, he left the world changed.

But Jesus was more than a role model, wise teacher, or even holy prophet. He was God in the flesh: fully human and fully God. The same God who created the universe chose to enter the world to end the separation between humanity and himself that sin had resulted in.

During his life on earth, Jesus fulfilled hundreds of prophecies, some of which were recorded thousands of years prior to his birth, which promised that God would appoint an extraordinary person to rescue his people from captivity. In addition to that, Jesus himself said quite clearly, and on several occasions, that he was this long-awaited "Messiah" or "Christ" (for example, John 4:25-26).

In every town and city that Jesus and his disciples visited, whether speaking to large crowds or intimate gatherings, his mission was the same: to tell everyone about the reign of God on earth, which he called the "kingdom of God" and which he himself had come to bring (Luke 4:43). Jesus invited hearers to receive this kingdom and with it a new value system and way of living. The miracles Jesus performed were signs to reveal God's powerful presence on earth and that he had chosen Jesus to establish this new way of life.

During Jesus' life and ministry, countless men and women would come to believe in him. Jesus was not offering a new religion but something entirely different. He was giving people the opportunity to leave their old selves behind and receive a new life through him. Jesus did not call people to fix themselves, get right, or do better. He knew that it was not possible and that the pursuit of it was exhausting. Instead, he called them—and he calls us—to place their trust in him and accept God's gift to humankind: what the Bible calls "grace."

## JESUS IS THE GRACE OF GOD

Grace. It's a popular concept across various fields— from psychology to spirituality to theology. While definitions vary, one word that ties them together may be this: kindness. I think of grace as the tangible expression of undeserved kindness. You extend grace to a friend who forgot your birthday. Or you extend grace to yourself for forgetting her birthday. God extends grace to us for something far more serious: falling short of his perfect standard.

You see, God commands us to be perfect. That might sound unreasonable. Doesn't God know we can't be perfect? He does. Don't we live in an imperfect world? We do. But remember, this is not how God designed the world or us to be. Yet Jesus makes it very clear: "Be perfect, therefore, as your heavenly Father is perfect" (Matthew 5:48).

This perfection is obeying God's law, which Jesus summed up in this way: *Love God with everything you have and love others as much as you love yourself* (Matthew 12:30-31). If this seems unachievable to you, you're right. In fact, the Bible tells us in the book of Romans:

*All have sinned and fall short of the glory of God.*
*(Romans 3:23)*

Nevertheless, God is unwavering about sin and its consequences. When sin entered the world, it created a chasm between Creator and creation. Connected to God, the source of life and truth, we are able to thrive inwardly, in our souls—knowing, believing, and walking in the truth. But disconnection from the source brings death—spiritual death and, eventually, physical death. "For the wages of sin is death, but the gift of God is eternal life in Christ Jesus our Lord" (6:23).

God commands us to be perfect. But he doesn't leave us in our failure. Because he is gracious, he also gives us the means to meet his standard. In compassion, love, and kindness, God gave us Jesus. God's love is so great that he made a way for us to live and thrive despite our sin: when we believe and trust in Jesus (paraphrasing John 3:16).

This is how the Bible puts it: "God made him who had no sin to be sin for us, so that in him we might become the righteousness of God" (2 Corinthians 5:21). Jesus lived a perfect life, connected to his Father in heaven. When he died on the cross, it was as though he swapped places with us; he experienced *our* death and disconnection so that we can experience *his* life and relationship with God. So we are made righteous—right with God—not through our efforts but through trusting in Christ's death on the cross.

You might know an old hymn called "Amazing Grace." The song is right; grace *is* amazing. God extends his lovingkindness towards you not because you have done anything to earn it but because he desires you to have it. All that we have to do to receive his grace is to turn from going our own direction and turn towards him—what the Bible means by "repent and believe" (Mark 1:15).

While God's grace is a free gift to us, it cost Jesus his life. However, the story didn't end there. Central to the message of Christianity is that Jesus returned to life after death. His body was placed in a tomb, and three days later, the tomb was empty. More than 500 witnesses claimed to have seen him, along with his disciples, who spent 40 days with a Jesus who was very much alive, after which he ascended into heaven (Acts 1:9).

Jesus' miraculous resurrection opened a new chapter for humanity. Whereas each of us is born physically alive but spiritually dead, the Bible tells us that there is a second birth available, whereby we gain spiritual life through Christ. When we repent and believe in Jesus, he sends his Spirit to live in us and make us new.

*Therefore, if anyone is in Christ, the new creation has
come. The old has gone, the new is here.*
*(2 Corinthians 5:17)*

Those who trust in Jesus have a new nature, which
allows us to love, trust, and experience life with God.

## GOD'S GRACE SETS US FREE

There are a lot of fancy theological words for what Jesus
accomplished on the cross: atonement, propitiation,
redemption, reconciliation. Bible scholars spend a
lifetime trying to grasp the full depth and meaning of
his grace—and with good reason. At the same time, the
gospel message is wonderfully simple: Jesus set us free
(Galatians 5:1).

What does it mean to be free? In the United States,
we talk about freedom in the sense of personal
autonomy: having the ability to do as we please. It
means being able to choose the kind of life we want
to live. When you are free, you are not forced to live
beneath your potential. You can reach as high and go
as far as you want. There are no limits to what you can
do or who you can become.

Biblical freedom means being able to become who
God has created you to be and live life as he intends.
Sin stands in the way of that. Our false beliefs about
God, ourselves, and others mean that we are constantly
making the wrong choices. But the good news is that
if you're trusting in Jesus, he's broken the power of
sin to hold you captive—spiritually, mentally, and
emotionally. Your sinful thoughts and feelings no
longer have to control your life. You can find inner

peace, despite your outward circumstances. In Jesus, our souls find rest.

In fact, Jesus defeated the enemy of our soul, Satan, who caused humanity to fall in the first place with his deception and lies, and who has been lying to us ever since (John 8:44). Those who believe the gospel have help to recognize and defeat the lies of the enemy, which cause chaos and confusion. While false beliefs keep us in bondage, Jesus said the truth will set you free (v 32).

God's grace sets you free to live a transformed life:

- free from the need to do and be enough

- free from the pressure to figure it all out

- free from the opinions and expectations of others

- free to let go of the past

- free to live with hope for the future

God can change you from the inside out. He can touch your heart and awaken your spirit. Whereas you were once blind to the truth, his grace enables you to finally see it.

And while a profound change has happened, a new life in Christ may not feel entirely different, at least initially. You see, salvation is both an immediate reality and also a lifetime journey. As we seek to obey God, we're called to "continue to work out your salvation with fear and trembling, for it is God who works in you to will and to act in order to fulfill his good purpose" (Philippians 2:12-13). God accepts us exactly as we are because of Jesus; but then he gradually works to change us, so we become like Jesus.

As a new Christian, I wish someone had told me that while my spiritual condition had changed—once and for all—my heart and mind had to be continually renewed. It's as we continuously align ourselves with the truth of God that we live out the new life Jesus has secured for us. We are made new at once, but we are also becoming newer every day.

## NO INSTANT RESULTS

When I turned to Jesus and received salvation, I was excited to kick off my brand new life. For the first few weeks into my Christian journey, I was "walking on sunshine," as the song says. I found myself thinking about Jesus, how special I felt to be chosen by him, wondering what he was telling all his friends about me... Okay, not that last part. But seriously, I was smitten. It felt like the clouds had parted and I finally understood what this whole life thing was about.

I bought a new study Bible, highlighters in assorted colors, sticky notes, and a journal. It was as though I was my 10-year-old self again, excited about the start of middle school: everything I would learn, the experiences I would treasure, and who I would grow to become.

But as the months went by, life felt more or less the same. Actually, life started to feel harder. I still had moments of being controlling, demanding, and impatient. Except now I felt worse about it because I knew that was no longer how I should be.

I was trying to do all the right things and stay away from all the wrong things, and it was exhausting. I thought that maybe I wasn't trying hard enough or didn't want Jesus in my life badly enough.

I see now that I was trying to self-help my way to God. I was approaching Christianity like I did other goals in my life—with focus, determination, and hard work—thinking I would find success. It would take me a long time to understand that I could not achieve the things of God through effort or willpower.

Living and looking like Jesus is not the product of a carefully crafted to-do list, excellent time-management skills, or having the commitment levels of a marathoner in training. We grow, change, and become who God has called us to be by his power, not our own.

It's God's grace that changes us. Yet we still have a role to play and a decision to make.

## EMBRACING GRACE

God gave us Jesus so that we could meet his perfect standard.

## MEMORY VERSE

*God made him who had no sin to be sin for us, so that in him we might become the righteousness of God.*
*(2 Corinthians 5:21)*

# CHAPTER 4

# THE DILEMMA

*"You cannot not make a decision."*

**Anonymous**

It was two days before my 30th birthday. I was sitting in my office when my cell phone rang. Immediately, I recognized the number and jumped out of my chair to close the door. Three rounds of interviews, writing tests, and reference checks—and here we were. I had even written my resignation letter, end date and all.

Six years after coming to Christ in church that Sunday, it seemed like God was taking me on the scenic route to the life of my dreams. But this was the call that would usher in a new season.

"We really want to thank you..." She didn't have to finish her sentence. I already knew. Before the call had even ended, despair had hit.

This time was supposed to be different. This was *my* time. I just knew this job was the blessing God had in store for me—until it wasn't.

Over the previous few years, I had watched girlfriends get married, become mothers, get promotions, and start businesses—seemingly knocking it all out the park. Meanwhile, I was coming to terms with the end of a decade-long relationship, feeling stuck in a job with no upward mobility, living in a house I bought that, it turned out, did not make me happy, with no clue about how to find or build the life I had been longing for.

I had always been good at setting and achieving goals. As a child, I learned what worked and applied it—and, well, it worked. My diligence was rewarded with honor rolls and honor societies, varsity letters, sorority letters, scholarships, and graduate assistantships.

I thought that if I had accomplished all of this *before* giving my life to Jesus, then surely I was going to experience so much more after coming to Christ. I wasn't naïve enough to think that becoming a Christian would make *all* my dreams come true—but I thought that Jesus plus time, dedication, and effort would tip the scales in my favor.

But six years after saying, "I do" to Jesus, I did not feel any closer to the life I desperately wanted or the person I knew I could be.

That was six years of Sunday services and Bible studies, tithes and offerings, countless devotionals, fasting, praying, serving, and trying my best to live right. Clearly, I was doing something wrong. It was like all the *real* believers knew how Christianity worked and I didn't. Or maybe they felt the same way I did but were too reverential to file a complaint with God. Whatever it was, the fact remained: being a Christian was not living up to my expectations.

Maybe that's where you're at right now. You've made the sacrifices to put God first, and yet life feels harder than ever. Perhaps you've prayed for purpose and direction, and God seems silent. Or maybe it seems like everyone's dreams are coming true but yours.

Being unable to see God working can feel discouraging and painful. All relationships have their struggles and strains, including a relationship with God.

Looking back now, I see that my expectations were impossible. Not because my desires were too hard for God but because I was trying to fit Jesus into a box: one heavily influenced by the ways of the world.

## THE WAYS OF THE WORLD

Those of us who live in the West, particularly the US, exist in a world that prides itself on hard work and achievement. We grow up believing that if you want something, you go out and make it happen. We believe that our success rides on how smart, capable, disciplined, and driven we are. The busier we are, the more important we feel. If we're not rising and grinding, booked and busy, then we can't be serious about life.

Doing a good job makes us feel worthy, and doing a bad job makes us question our worth. The only thing standing in our way is ourselves, we think. While this belief stirs up a fair amount of anxiety, it also gives us something we desperately want: a sense of control.

*Sure, I'm stressed and burned out, but at least I get to decide if I sink or swim*, we think. We dare not consider the alternative: that life doesn't happen the way we want, no matter how hard we work or how phenomenal we are.

For those of us who are Christians, we even assume we're in control of our spiritual lives. Salvation may "belong to the Lord" (Revelation 7:10), but we commend ourselves for choosing to believe in it—as though we could desire God without God enabling us to.

Or maybe we give him the glory but not the control. "Thank you, Jesus, for saving me, but I'll take it from here." That was me.

I knew the change I wanted in my life, and now I had Jesus to make it happen. I didn't realize it, but Jesus had become a means to an end. I curbed profanity, hoping God would answer my prayers affirmatively. I swore off sexual activity so that God would send me a husband quicker. I was cheerful and charitable, hoping that God was taking notes. On the outside, I was honoring God, but my motivation was the fulfillment of *my* desires.

I was also trying to earn God's favor. Deep down, I hoped my strong work ethic, positive attitude, and accomplishments would make the case for a life promotion. But that's how the world operates, not God. Divine grace, if you remember, is given not because we are good but because God is good.

And that's so much better than the alternative. If you believe that you must be good enough to have a full and satisfying life, you will always be working. What you did to earn it is what you will have to do to keep it. But God wants to release you from the pressure of having to achieve your way through life.

The Bible tells us that God will take care of everything we need based on the blessings that come from Jesus (Philippians 4:19). "What's the catch?" you ask. Well, he may go about it differently than you expect or desire. There's also a good chance that his plans may not perfectly align with your vision board or timeline.

If that is the case, what do you do? Do you hand over the reins and trust God? Or do you dig in your heels and double down on your plans?

Friends, we have a dilemma on our hands.

## GOD'S PLAN OR YOUR PLAN?

One key aspect of Christianity is the concept of surrender. When we say, "Yes" to Jesus, we let go of our plans, desires, and our very selves, trusting God with all of it.

The idea of yielding control to a "higher power" is practiced in various religious and spiritual traditions. In his best-selling book, *The Power of Now*, Eckhart Tolle teaches that we cannot fully experience and appreciate life unless we release resistance and learn to surrender. Spiritual teachers like Tolle tell us that a surrendered life is one of freedom, contentment, and peace.

For the Christian believer, though, we surrender not to a universal force but a personal God—one who has proved himself, through Jesus, to be trustworthy and good. This act of surrender is choosing to give back to Jesus the new life he's secured for you: a daily decision that is repeated for a lifetime.

By "decision," I mean that it is a choice. God will not force you to give up ownership of your life, your decision-making, or your plans. Jesus said, "Whoever wants to be my disciple must deny themselves and take up their cross daily and follow me" (Luke 9:23).

When I set out to follow Jesus, I was convinced that God's ways would make my dreams come true. However, I was trying to follow Jesus *and* hold on to my plans.

Despite the frustration of not getting what I wanted, I wasn't willing to let go.

I believed God's plans were good. But were they better than what I desired? Would his plans satisfy me, even if they came at the expense of my own?

If we are to surrender to Jesus, that's the underlying question we must consider: is having Jesus, alone, enough?

## IS JESUS ENOUGH?

When it comes to life, we want our gains to be greater than the pain. We hope the new job will be worth the longer hours and additional stress. We hope the vacation will be worth the layovers and crowded airports. We hope our portfolio will be worth the investment.

While this is the way of the world, I brought this mindset into my relationship with Jesus. I wanted a tangible return. If I had to give up everything, I needed to see the benefits not one day in heaven but in the here and now.

In the book of Ephesians, Paul lists the spiritual blessings of a relationship with God through Jesus: salvation, adoption into God's family, acceptance, redemption, forgiveness, insight into God's will, the Holy Spirit, and an inheritance to come (1:4-14).

Yet those weren't the benefits I was looking for. Instead, I had a whole list of goals and milestones that I was eager to check off. But, as the time went by—year seven, year eight, and then year nine—my destination felt further and further away.

I was tired of riding in the backseat, waiting on God. So I did what came easy: I took control. I spent my last year in Atlanta trying to transform myself and my life. I ran a half marathon, took improv classes, became a mentor, dropped gluten, and cut my hair off. I even got my first tattoo. That 12-month period was my last-ditch "Hail Mary" pass to Jesus, hoping for a victory.

But sitting at my dining-room table, on the first day of the first month of 2014, I felt anything but a champion. It was then that I decided that the crazy idea posed by a friend several months earlier wasn't so crazy after all. I was going to move to New York.

If there was a place that could awaken my best self and inspire me to greatness, it was the City of Dreams. I had tried Jesus but wasn't convinced that he was the only answer. I wanted true happiness, power, identity, and love. I was ready to live the life I imagined and taste and see what the Big Apple had to offer.

### EMBRACING GRACE
God will take care of everything you need through Jesus, who has an unlimited supply of blessings.

### MEMORY VERSE

*And my God will meet all your needs according to the riches of his glory in Christ Jesus. (Philippians 4:19)*

# PART TWO

# Searching

# CHAPTER 5

# DON'T WORRY, BE HAPPY

*"Happiness cannot come from without.*
*It must come from within."*[5]

**Helen Keller**

I moved to Brooklyn, New York in April of 2014. A friend referred me for a job, and three months later, I was packing my bags, organizing a garage sale, and saying my goodbyes. My loved ones were super supportive—impressed, even, by my leap of faith. Deep down, I knew there was more for me to experience and become. Like Disney's Snow Queen Elsa and other trailblazers before her, I was ready to venture into the unknown.

Something inside of me had awakened: the belief that anything was possible. I had felt similarly during those early seasons of getting to know Jesus. I had felt alive, purposeful, and just plain good. But that hadn't lasted. So now, I was looking for other options. Perhaps there was more to know: more complete answers to be found elsewhere—to be found in New York, even.

For one thing, I was going to be happier. You know that one person who just seems naturally happy. She is cheerful and pleasant even under stress, approaching life with an enviable combination of optimism and hope. When I turned to Jesus nearly ten years prior, I had thought that was going to be me. Except my moods were far more variable. I was happy, as long as things were going great. But when life handed me lemons, my attitude and perspective turned sour.

I was ready to kick the habit. I wanted more from life than bouts of happiness. I wanted the real thing. I wanted real, sustainable, deep-down joy. My guess is that you do too.

## THE PURSUIT OF HAPPINESS

There is a happiness imperative that runs the world. It's ingrained in the very fiber of America; as the Declaration of Independence states, we've been entitled to life, liberty, and "the pursuit of *happiness*." So, what exactly is happiness? And how do we get it?

Psychologist and researcher Sonja Lyubomirsky, in her book *The How of Happiness*, defines happiness as "the experience of joy, contentment, or positive well-being, combined with a sense that one's life is good, meaningful, and worthwhile."[6] For a lot of people, happiness is tied to the pursuit of particular outcomes. You will be happy when you get the new job, meet "the one," get in shape, or finish the book. But not soon after you achieve your goal, another desire pops up in its place, holding happiness hostage. Or worse, what you thought would make you happy leaves you disappointed or disillusioned.

Yet self-help books everywhere tell us that happiness is available—that we can create and control our own happiness. We can't always control the environment. But happiness is different. Happiness, we read, is a choice. Dr. Lyubomirsky, for example, says that while 10% of happiness is due to our individual circumstances, a whopping 40% is due to our personal outlook. The other half is simply genetics (so there really are naturally happy people!).

As I began this new chapter in New York, I figured that if happiness could be practiced and learned, I was the girl for the job. There were three big ideas that guided my thoughts and inspired my actions: 1) giving life a "yes," 2) being positive, and 3) being mindful.

## 1. YES, AND YOLO

Think about a time when you were really happy. Where were you and what were you doing? I think back to a trip with my cousins to Italy: riding in a boat along the Amalfi Coast, with the sun shining, birds singing, and the wind kissing my face.

It's one thing to feel happy on vacation. But much of life is more mundane. So, what if there was a way to experience new and exciting things more often—to seize every day to learn about ourselves, others, and the world around us? Surely that would unlock a more satisfying and happy existence?

When I moved to New York, I wanted to do better with making the most of every day. So, when I stumbled upon Shonda Rhimes' best-seller *Year of Yes*, I found the inspiration I needed. In her 2015 best-seller, Rhimes examines how saying yes for one year to everything that scared her changed her life.

Giving life a big fat "yes" seemed like a worthwhile challenge. I was no longer going to be what or who held me back. I was going to live every day to the fullest. I was ready to "*carpe* the *diem*" and begin YOLO-ing the moment.

I said yes to an invitation to join a semester-long workshop on the politics of gender and sexuality. The old me would have needed dozens of questions answered and at least a semester to decide. But I was turning over a new leaf! Saying yes allowed me to meet all kinds of interesting people, and I even gained a dear and lifelong friend. Sitting in class, hearing different points of view, and connecting with others was enjoyable; it made me feel alive.

At the same time, my "seize the day" philosophy created pressure to make and sustain my satisfaction. I found myself having to check off item after item to find enjoyment. I mean, how many parks, plays, brunches, bookstores, and museums can a person frequent? The pursuit of happiness was costing me, in more ways than one.

At some point between learning how to do magic and American Sign Language, I ran out of to-dos. There had to be another way! If 40% of happiness was based on outlook, perhaps the answer wasn't doing the right things but thinking the right things.

## 2. BEING POSITIVE

We live in a culture that values positivity. We don't like feeling bad, and many of us feel bad for even feeling bad. Self-help strategies aim to help by encouraging us to release that which no longer serves us. We read that we should focus on the destination, not on the difficulties. After all, happiness is a state of mind. We can think our way to happiness. And one of the ways to do that, we're told, is to practice positive affirmations.

Going online, I found affirmations promising to improve my mood, raise my confidence, foster gratitude, and more. I also created my own, adding them to a growing list in my journal. Every day, I committed myself to saying and "receiving" what I said.

*"I believe in myself and my abilities."*

*"I am meant to live a happy life."*

*"I accept that happiness is my true nature."*

*"I deserve all that is good."*

After about 30 days of telling myself that I was happy, successful, and worthy, I still felt the opposite. I was at a loss. Saying one thing but believing another did not convert my thoughts but instead created confusion. I couldn't shake the feeling that my affirmations—as good as they sounded—weren't exactly true. What's more, the idea that I was *supposed* to be positive all the time led me to judge myself for feeling anything negative. As a result, I started to hide or dismiss how I really felt. Unsurprisingly, being dishonest with myself and others did not bring me closer to happiness but took me further away.

Then I stumbled upon a new idea. I could choose to accept the reality of my situation and even myself. I could let go of how things were *supposed* to be and embrace how things simply were.

The next stop on my happiness search: mindfulness.

## 3. MINDING MY MIND

We spend a lot of time thinking about something other than what we are doing. One study from Harvard University found that we spend nearly half our waking hours (46.9%) thinking about things that have already happened or things that may never happen at all.[7] And our wandering minds are not making us very happy.

Enter mindfulness: the practice of bringing your full attention to what is happening in the present moment. Something about it resonated with me. It didn't involve pretending to be happy or needing things to be a certain way. It was all about accepting things as they were and being content with your life and yourself. That sounded great. So I got to work.

I learned the Five Senses game and played it at the park: *I see the tree, feel the wind, hear the birds, smell the grass, and taste the water from the fountain.* I slowed down while eating, taking in the tastes, textures, and temperatures of my food. Through mindfulness, I discovered that hearing birds makes me smile and a dash of lemon makes everything taste better. I began to find satisfaction in the simple things.

Next on my list was mindfulness's big sister: meditation. Since both spiritual teachers and neuroscientists agreed that it was beneficial for well-being, I figured there had to be something to it.

For two months, almost every morning, I committed to meditating. Some days it was just for a few minutes and other days for up to half an hour. I imagined lying on the beach or in a hammock in the park. I counted my breath. I visualized words and wrote them in my head, one letter at a time. There were days when I wondered if any of it was working. Then there were days when I would feel less worry and unmistakable peace.

Until, that is, I boarded the New York City subway to begin my daily commute from Crown Heights to the Financial District. Although just eight stops, it was enough to make the Buddha himself question his past life choices.

In the end, mantras and meditation, like my other happiness strategies, brought some positive effects, but they were not the answer. Searching for happiness brought me to the truth that seeking it apart from God is a search done in vain. We all want to experience joy, well-being, and satisfaction. The good news is that happiness is very much a part of the Christian life.

## GOD'S THOUGHTS ON THE MATTER

When you think about God's character and nature, what words come to mind? *Powerful*, *creative*, and *wise*, perhaps. But what about *happy*? Is God, to go back to Dr. Lyubomirsky's definition from earlier, currently enjoying an "experience of joy, contentment, or positive well-being?"

I'd say the answer is "Yes." Given his holiness, glory, good deeds, and good works, how could he not be happy? To be sure, God doesn't experience emotions in the way that we humans do. While our happiness—or lack of it—is often the result of external circumstances, God is happy in himself, all the time. The word the Bible often uses to describe that is "blessed"—meaning "perfectly fulfilled in every good thing."[8] God is "blessed forever" (2 Corinthians 11:31, ESV) and is "the blessed and only Ruler" (1 Timothy 6:15).

God is happy forever and always. We also see this in the Trinity: the idea that there is one God, who exists in three Persons: the Father, Son, and Holy Spirit. The Father takes eternal pleasure in the Son (Matthew 17:5), and the Son is pleased and happy in the Father's love (John 17:13). They have full and complete joy in each other through the power of the Holy Spirit and have so since long before humanity was ever created.

God is happy—and the good news means that he has designed us and desires us to be happy too. Which brings us back to the question: how?

## THE ULTIMATE SOURCE OF HAPPINESS

We can find happiness in a lot of good things: time spent with loved ones, a good meal, music, or seeing the world. These are all sources of happiness—but they are designed to point us back to the ultimate and original source: God, who made them. The most complete joy and happiness is found in relationship with him: "You will fill me with joy in your presence, with eternal pleasures at your right hand" (Psalm 16:11).

Think of it this way. I have a picture on my refrigerator that makes me happy. I like the bright colors and bold shapes. But what really makes me smile is when I think of my niece, who drew it and gave it to me. I'm reminded of her sunny personality, her creativity, and her love for me. So the picture gives me a measure of happiness, but that increases several-fold when it causes me to think of its creator—and my joy increases still further when I actually spend time with her. The same is true with the good things that we enjoy. They are gifts to us from the God who loves us, and they reflect something about his character—and it's in remembering him that our enjoyment increases.

The Bible is clear that we find happiness in belonging to God, through Jesus. "Happy are the people whose God is the LORD!" (Psalm 144:15, NKJV). In relationship with Jesus, you can experience the satisfaction and happiness you are looking for.

While the world tells us that whatever makes us happy is good, the Bible tells us that whatever is good makes us happy. We read in the book of Psalms, "The precepts of the LORD are right, giving joy to the heart" (19:8). The trouble comes when we desire happiness more than God and don't believe that happiness comes *through* God. When that happens, we can end up wandering away from God and what pleases him in favor of what is pleasing and desirable to us.

If complete joy is to be found in God's presence, then separation from him kills joy. The irony is that many people believe that *God* is a killjoy, taking away all the pleasure, satisfaction, and fun we stand to gain. Nothing could be further from the truth. God is happy, and he offers you a happiness that the world can't provide (John 16:22). It's a happiness the world cannot stain or steal—which is great news, especially if you find yourself in a place right now that feels anything but happy.

## HAPPINESS 2.0: JOY

There's a refrain I remember hearing as a child, spoken by elders in song and praise: "This joy I have, the world didn't give it, and the world can't take it away." What they were saying was that their happiness was not determined by their external environment. The world and what it offered was not the source of their happiness. God was. This enduring, unaffected happiness is what Christians sometimes call "joy."

God himself rejoices over his people:

*He will take great delight in you; in his love he will no longer rebuke you, but will rejoice over you with singing. (Zephaniah 3:17)*

And we, as God's people, are commanded to rejoice in him: "Rejoice in the Lord always. I will say it again: Rejoice!" (Philippians 4:4). Rejoicing is to happen at all times—not sometimes or on occasion but always. But how is that possible?

Paul provides our answer: that Christians are to rejoice in *the Lord*. And God doesn't change, even when our circumstances do. Our joy is based on what Jesus has done, is doing, and will do in our lives—how he has saved us from sin, walks with us by his Spirit, and will one day bring us home to be with him forever, in a world free from pain and sorrow. Knowing Jesus, the believer is filled with "inexpressible and glorious joy" (1 Peter 1:8). We experience the joy of the Lord!

I witnessed this joy first-hand when I stepped onto the campus of The African SOUP School in 2023, as a member of its US Board of Directors. Located in rural eastern Uganda, the SOUP provides high-quality education and health services to strengthen the local community. All around me, I saw children learning, laughing, and enjoying life in humble circumstances. As I spent more time with them and their teachers, the source of their joy became clear. "Praise the Lord," one of the students exclaimed as he introduced himself to the class. "Hallelujah," the room responded.

God is able to impart joy to your soul, no matter what your circumstances are. In fact, joy is part of the fruit of the Holy Spirit (Galatians 5:22). Connected to Christ, you can have supernatural joy. That is not to say that sadness or sorrow is not real. Instead, you can endure difficult times and emotions because "the joy of the LORD is your strength" (Nehemiah 8:10).

## THREE KEYS TO TRUE HAPPINESS

God created you to be happy, commands that you be happy, and stands ready to fill you with deep, abiding happiness. Yet happiness is not an automatic reality, even for believers. God's path to happiness requires that we walk it out. Thankfully, the Bible teaches us how to do that, aided by God's grace and power. Here are three places to start—habits that turn the self-help advice I followed on its head.

### 1. SAY YES TO GOD: *LISTEN TO WHAT HE SAYS AND ACT ON IT*

*Praise the LORD!*

*How joyful are those who fear the LORD*
  *and delight in obeying his commands.*
                                    *(Psalm 112:1, NLT)*

For a while, I sought happiness by saying yes to anything and everything that came my way, even those things that took me outside of my comfort zone. But we'll find a deeper happiness in seeking out what God says in his word and putting it into practice. The Christian life is not one of passive retreat but of intentional action, as we set out to follow Jesus and serve those around us—not to earn good things but as an overflow of the grace he's *already* shown us.

This may well take us outside of our comfort zone. It may even feel painful at times. But this verse and others promise that obedience leads to joy. Jesus came to give us life to the full (John 10:10)—not merely a full schedule.

## 2. PRACTICE GOD-CENTERED AFFIRMATION: *ACKNOWL-EDGE, CELEBRATE, AND HONOR GOD IN ALL YOU DO*

*Then they worshiped [Jesus] and returned to Jerusalem with great joy. (Luke 24:52)*

I realize now that my daily positive affirmations were pointing in the wrong direction. We'll find the greatest joy and freedom when we take our eyes off ourselves and set them on the one who is worthy of our worship: the Lord God. It's what our human hearts have been designed to do, right from the start.

I can think of no better way to start the day than by telling God how awesome he is—not because he needs it but because we do. And gathering with other believers each Sunday to praise God together feeds our joy too.

And the affirmations run two ways: when we open his word, we hear God tell us how precious we are to him, despite our sin and weakness. That remains true—whether we believe it or not—and is enough to sustain us on any subway commute.

### 3. BE MINDFUL OF THE GIVER: *REMAIN CONNECTED AND IN COMMUNION WITH GOD*

*You have made known to me the paths of life; you will*
*fill me with joy in your presence. (Acts 2:28)*

Mindfulness taught me to enjoy the things in front of me, instead of always passing by in a rush—and for that, I'm grateful. But there's another important step. We'll find joy as we intentionally receive the things in front of us as gifts from God's hand—as we slow down enough to see his kindness behind the things that we enjoy.

Today, slow down to savor one good thing: a taste, a sound, a sight, or a smell. Enjoy it for what it is. And then turn your mind to God, who created it. Let that thing remind you of his character and his love. Receive it as a good gift from him and say thank you!

### A HAPPY STATE OF MIND: CONTENTMENT

God has designed our hearts to experience joy and gladness—and that is possible even as we go through difficult times. The New Testament author Paul speaks to this reality as he writes that he is "sorrowful, yet always rejoicing" (2 Corinthians 6:10). Another translation says, "Our hearts ache, but we always have joy" (NLT).

Paul knew suffering well, having been beaten, imprisoned, shipwrecked, and more, all in the course of telling people about Christ. At the same time, Paul felt joy because he recognized his own suffering was momentary, and he chose to view his life from a spiritual perspective. He delighted in Jesus more than anything else. He was satisfied with his life situation, accepting the will of God and trusting in Christ. Simply put, Paul was content.

Contentment is having peace on a sunny day and in the midst of your biggest, most difficult storm. Here's how Paul puts it:

> For I have learned how to be content with whatever I have. I know how to live on almost nothing or with everything. I have learned the secret of living in every situation, whether it is with a full stomach or empty, with plenty or little. For I can do everything through Christ, who gives me strength.
>
> (Philippians 4:11-13, NLT)

Here's what I find encouraging: Paul *learned* to be content. That means he didn't start out that way. His contentment grew over time as he walked with Jesus daily, receiving his joy and his strength. This growth is possible for you and me as well.

The Bible is clear about where contentment, joy, and happiness lie: in Jesus. You don't have to search for happiness. You will find it when you seek God and obey him in faith. You don't have to maintain your happiness. God will sustain it as you continue to trust, obey, and seek him.

You don't have to go looking for happiness because it is an inside job. Inside of every believer lives the delightful, cheerful, and joyful Spirit of God. If you're trusting in him, then he is working to grow your joy today.

## EMBRACING GRACE
In relationship with Jesus, you can experience the satisfaction and happiness you are looking for.

## MEMORY VERSE

*Taste and see that the LORD is good;*
*blessed is the one who takes refuge in him.*

*(Psalm 34:8)*

# CHAPTER 6

# POWER UP

*"Smooth seas do not make skillful sailors."*

**Unknown Proverb**

On September 24, 1988, Jackie Joyner-Kersee won gold at the Summer Olympics in Seoul, Korea, setting two world records in the heptathlon and long jump. Incredibly, her heptathlon record was still on the books in 2023 when she was inducted into the International Sports Hall of Fame. Joyner-Kersee is considered one of the greatest women athletes of all time.

Yet her path to greatness was not without obstacles or setbacks. Growing up in East St. Louis, Illinois, Joyner-Kersee witnessed first-hand the damaging effects of poverty on her family and community. During her first year of college, she was rocked by the sudden death of her mother, and as a star athlete at the University of California, Los Angeles (UCLA), she was diagnosed with asthma. In her career, she faced multiple injuries that forced her to withdraw from competitions, and her reputation was attacked with allegations of steroid use. Yet, despite it all, she excelled.

Joyner-Kersee's story is rare, yet it illustrates a common desire: we all want to exercise power over our situation and accomplish something worthwhile. While you might not aspire to win Olympic gold, my guess is that you have your own goals and dreams. Maybe there's something right now that you're hoping or praying to make possible. You've been working at it for a while now and are starting to wonder if it will ever happen. It's tough waiting on your time or your turn—when you look at your circumstances and nothing seems to be changing. Can you relate—or is it just me? Disappointment and delays can leave you feeling stuck, unable or unsure of how to move forward.

The question is: Where do we find the power to make things happen? Is there a better way to accomplish our desires?

## THE PURSUIT OF POWER

All around, people are looking for the power to make their dreams come true. Inherent in the philosophy of self-help is the belief that we can change things about ourselves and our lives. And oftentimes, we can. God has given human beings a brain to think with and a will to choose with, as well as various personal qualities and strengths.

Experts in self-improvement tell us that we are able to cultivate and unleash this inner power with the right mindsets and habits. Author and high-performance coach Brendon Burchard invites readers to reclaim their power in his *New York Times'* best-selling book *The Motivation Manifesto*. Burchard believes it is our ability to choose our attitude and actions that makes us powerful. He writes that "wrong thinking and weak wills" prevent people from progressing toward their goals.[9] According to Burchard, we have the ability to "bend reality to our own preferences, crafting the lives we desire through disciplined learning and initiative."[10]

Burchard is not the first person to contemplate how our thoughts affect reality. How much power do we have in our minds to shape the circumstances around us? This "mind-matter" connection is a hotbed of various self-help teachings and techniques, promising to transform every aspect of our lives. During my own search for power, I explored two of them: the "Law of Attraction" and "Energy Alignment."

## 1. MANIFESTING YOUR DESIRES

Searching for books on the Law of Attraction, I stumbled pretty quickly on what is perhaps the most successful of them all: Rhonda Byrne's 2006 best-seller *The Secret*. (The endorsement of media mogul Oprah Winfrey certainly helped its success.) In *The Secret*, Byrne teaches that a person's thoughts have the power to direct and influence the universe. The idea is that your thoughts magnetically attract things of the same frequency; therefore, you attract what you think about the most.

Initially, when I learned about the Law of Attraction, I didn't see it as incompatible with faith in Jesus but more of an add-on or enhancement. In fact, some of what I read sounded Christian-like. Byrne's three-step process for attracting what you want—ask, believe, and receive—sounded awfully similar to Jesus' words in the book of Matthew: "If you believe, you will receive whatever you ask for in prayer" (Matthew 21:22).

According to Byrne, by consciously choosing our thoughts, we can change our lives. That was enough to get me going.

I cracked open a brand new journal and committed to the path for six weeks. The first thing to do, according to Byrne, was to list the things I wanted to manifest. I wrote a few things down, including a serious relationship with a guy I was seeing at the time, and securing a $30,000 donation for the nonprofit I was working for.

Not even a week after making my declaration, I learned about a fundraising event that a couple of trustees were hosting just four weeks away. It seemed like things were aligning!

Following Byrne's advice, I visualized the night and how it would all go down. I would float across the room, my charisma and charm opening up hearts and wallets. Everyone at the party would wonder who this dynamic, brilliant young woman was, and I'd collect pledge after pledge, check after check.

The reality could not have been more different. There I was, staring out the window of this jaw-dropping Upper East Side penthouse, wondering what emergency I could fabricate in order to hop on the elevator and disappear into the night. I tried to think positively, believe, and receive. But the universe was not responding. Instead of pledge cards and checks, I left the event that night with frustration and disappointment.

For weeks I had tried to put the principles into practice. But there were no miraculous donations and no real progress in my "situationship." In fact, that particular guy ended up disappearing.

Did the Law of Attraction not work? Scouring the

internet, I found a long list of reasons why it might have been user error. Was I was too desperate, fearful, impatient, and wedded to the outcome? "Yes, all of the above," I thought.

To be told that I had to address all these areas before I could attract my desires was unsettling, to say the least. Did having the life of my dreams require me to be perfect? There had to be another way. I would soon discover another promising principle.

## 2. GETTING BETTER ALIGNED

The Law of Attraction suggests positive energy is required for positive experiences. "Energy Alignment" is a practice designed to activate the body's energy system, by focusing on seven *"chakras"* located in different parts of the body. According to a strand of ancient Hindu teaching, opening a person's *chakras* allows them to think and feel better, which can improve the manifesting process.

While Energy Alignment was new terrain for me, I knew someone who could help: a trained Reiki practitioner I'd met through a coaching program. I reached out to set up a time to talk.

Two weeks later, I was lying on my living room floor, halfway through a virtual Reiki session. For the first part of the call, we discussed my mental and emotional well-being and completed a guided meditation. During the last 30 minutes, I relaxed, listening to music, after which the practitioner shared what she felt on an "energetic level."

She concluded that I had difficulty making decisions, wrestled with fear of failure, and struggled with the need for control and answers. She wasn't wrong. She told me to explore my third *chakra*, the solar plexus, thought to be the center of personal power. She suggested I try shaking up my routine, surrounding myself with the color yellow, repeating positive affirmations, and strengthening my core and digestive muscles.

After two weeks of affirming myself, doing sit-ups, eating pineapples, and taking a different route to work, I gave up. Not because it was impractical, which it was. Not because it was unbiblical, which it was. Not because it didn't work for me, which it didn't.

I let it go because I was tired. I didn't feel more capable, strong, or grounded. I felt incapable, confused, and overwhelmed.

In my search for power, I had learned that relying on my own strength was a high-stakes, high-pressure situation. When you put your full trust and confidence in yourself, there's little room for error or rest.

But thankfully, there is another option. There is power available—the best kind of power—found in the ultimate source of power.

## GOD'S THOUGHTS ON THE MATTER

God is all-powerful and rules over everything in the universe. "Look up into the heavens. Who created all the stars? He brings them out like an army, one after another, calling each by its name. Because of his great power and incomparable strength, not a single one is missing" (Isaiah 40:26, NLT). In a world that sometimes feels as though it is spinning out of control, this is a truth that can keep us grounded. If you don't believe that there's a good, all-powerful God governing the universe, then it makes sense to scramble around looking for a lever that might possibly be the brakes. But if we take the Bible's message seriously, we'll be reassured that God's got the wheel.

More than that, the Bible also speaks of God giving power to those who put their faith in Jesus—and for a very particular purpose. "His divine power has given us everything we need for a godly life through our knowledge of him who called us by his own glory and goodness" (2 Peter 1:3).

We have God's power to live a "godly life." That's Christian-speak for living like Jesus—with the kind of love, kindness, courage, joy, and patience that he showed and more. God desires to grow and mature us spiritually, before and beyond any goal we hope to accomplish in our careers, marriages, businesses, or creative pursuits. If we're one of his people, this growth in godliness is his plan for our lives, and he has all the power we need to make it happen.

When we understand this, it's actually pretty humbling. We cannot be faithful to God without his power. We cannot resist temptation without his power. We cannot find joy in dark times without his power. But *with* God's power, our lives can demonstrate love, joy, peace, patience, and more. His power helps us live as we have been called.

God empowered my friend Brandon to live his life to the fullest in spite of an aggressive brain tumor. I met Brandon in 2012 after he courageously shared his story during a Sunday service at church. You'd expect a person in that situation to either sink into despair or focus inward, doing as much for themselves with what time they have. Yet, in the time I got to know Brandon, I saw him make the daily decision to inspire, encourage, and share his faith with others, trusting God every step of the way. "With God, all things are possible, and every day there are brand new possibilities ... Whatever it is, we can rely on God's strength to get us through our weakness," Brandon once shared on his blog.

Through God's power, Brandon was able to face a difficult journey and praise him through it all. Sadly, Brandon passed away in 2013 at the age of 26. He had wanted to leave a legacy, and he did. Brandon beautifully demonstrated the goodness of God and the greatness of his power. And that is what the Christian life is about.

The apostle Paul put it like this: "[The Lord] said to me, 'My grace is sufficient for you, for my power is made perfect in weakness'" (2 Corinthians 12:9). Whatever our circumstances—whether they are life-threatening like Brandon's or just frustratingly mundane—God's grace and his power provide us with everything we need to live a life of faith.

## THE POWER OF THE HOLY SPIRIT

Manifesting is all about harnessing your inner power to change an impersonal "universe." However, the Christian worldview says that powerful change happens as the personal God transforms our inner world. And the way he does that is through the presence of his Spirit.

The Holy Spirit is not a thing or force but a personal being. He is the third Person of the Holy Trinity (the idea we mentioned in chapter 5 that there is one God in three Persons). From the beginning of time, the Holy Spirit has played, and will continue to play, a vital role in the creation, redemption, and restoration of the world and everything in it, including you and me.

The night Jesus was arrested, he promised his disciples that he would not leave them alone but would send them the Holy Spirit (John 14:16). The Holy Spirit is not reserved for the holiest of Christians but is a gift to *all* who believe. Every person who places their faith in Jesus receives the precious Holy Spirit. His extraordinary power can accomplish far more than anything we could ever do on our own.

## FIVE WAYS THE HOLY SPIRIT EMPOWERS

Let's briefly consider five ways that the Holy Spirit is actively involved in the life of the believer—working in us, for us, and through us. As you read this list, pause and reflect on which particular areas you'd most like his help and power in at the moment.

### 1. THE POWER TO ACT WISELY

It's not always easy to know what God might be saying or doing in your life. The Holy Spirit, who is called the Spirit of truth (John 16:13), gives you knowledge and understanding of God's will as you pray, read his word, and talk with other believers. The Holy Spirit also helps you accomplish God's plans through your actions and decisions.

*If any of you lacks wisdom, you should ask God, who gives generously to all without finding fault, and it will be given to you. (James 1:15)*

## 2. THE POWER TO GROW

As we walk by the Spirit, our habits and attitudes begin to change. If you were once quick to quit, for example, God grows your patience and perseverance, so that you trust him and keep going. Or if before you tended towards jealousy and control in your relationships, the Spirit helps you to grow increasingly kind and at peace.

*But the fruit of the Spirit is love, joy, peace, forbearance, kindness, goodness, faithfulness, gentleness and self-control. (Galatians 5:22-23a)*

## 3. THE POWER TO HEAL

Sometimes, we may struggle because we are dealing with inward hurts. As a result, we may experience fear, frustration, defensiveness, and other hindrances to progress. But the Holy Spirit is present and available to help you along your journey of healing, in community with other believers; this often includes the help of trusted friends and pastors, as well as counselors and other professionals.

*For God has not given us a spirit of fear, but of power and of love and of a sound mind.*

*(2 Timothy 1:7, NKJV)*

## 4. THE POWER TO UNITE

There is a popular expression that says, "There is power in numbers." As believers, we are called to unite, and support and build one another up, as a spiritual family. The Holy Spirit helps us work together to accomplish the plans God has for us as individuals and as a church community. We all need people to pray for us, encourage us, and even correct us. We are stronger together.

*All the believers were one in heart and mind. No one claimed that any of their possessions was their own, but they shared everything they had. (Acts 4:32)*

## 5. THE POWER TO SERVE

God empowers every believer with spiritual gifts. When you receive salvation, you also receive divine giftings to fulfill God's purpose in your life, your church, and the world—that more people would come to know Jesus, for his glory. The Holy Spirit imparts gifts of teaching, serving, encouraging, leading, and so much more—even administration (1 Corinthians 12:28)! Joining God at work, doing what he's equipped you to do, is his definition of success.

*Each of you should use whatever gift you have received to serve others, as faithful stewards of God's grace in its various forms. (1 Peter 4:10)*

## WALKING IN STEP WITH THE SPIRIT

The power of the Holy Spirit is vital to the Christian life—and, thankfully, God's power is readily available to all who believe. The natural next question might be: how do we access this power?

While self-help offers strategies to cultivate personal power, it is God himself who empowers and equips us to accomplish everything he has planned. That's not to say you don't have a role to play. Your role is to entrust your life to the Lord—your hopes, desires, and goals—and, as you do so, to step out in faith and see what he's able to do with your efforts.

Paul puts it like this: "Since we live by the Spirit, let us keep in step with the Spirit" (Galatians 5:25). Paul is encouraging us to listen to God, allow him to lead, and acknowledge our total dependence on him. As we do that, God lifts the burden from us of having to figure out every detail of life and the pressure that this creates. Instead, we can focus on cultivating the fruit of the Spirit in whatever situation we're in: "love, joy, peace, forbearance, kindness, goodness, faithfulness, gentleness and self-control" (v 22-23). When we walk by the Spirit, we adjust our ways and our agenda to God's will and his ways. This isn't a one-and-done deal but a day-by-day thing.

I remember, a few years back, thinking about leaving a job. There didn't seem to be any more opportunities for me, and I was starting to feel restless. On top of that, I was watching peers secure promotions and significant salary increases by leaving their current jobs for new roles. I applied for a few jobs, and even got some interviews, but nothing was panning out. Feeling frustrated and unclear, I came across a particular Scripture one morning.

*See, I am doing a new thing! Now it springs up; do you not perceive it? I am making a way in the wilderness and streams in the wasteland. (Isaiah 43:19)*

This was the word God gave a prophet named Isaiah, expressing his promise to bring the Israelites out of captivity in Babylon and re-establish their home in

Jerusalem. I also knew it applied to me, as a follower of Jesus, because all the Old Testament prophecies find their ultimate fulfillment in him. Now, I wasn't in captivity, certainly. But I did feel stuck. And I didn't see anything "new" happening either. Perhaps God *was* doing something I couldn't perceive. I sensed the Holy Spirit telling my spirit to trust, wait, and see. And he gave me the power to do so.

And wouldn't you know, I got a new job... two years later. I think the "new thing" God was doing was bigger than a job. During that time, he taught me patience, humility, and contentment. He also gave me wisdom and experiences that I could use to encourage others waiting on their own season to change. In those years of waiting, he also helped me to form surprising new friendships, which I cherish to this day.

When we keep in step with the Spirit, he enables us to operate beyond our natural abilities. God wants to bless you well beyond the material. Through his power, you can walk out the life he has called you to live and accomplish what he has called you to do.

## MORE THAN WE CAN IMAGINE

God has abundant power and generously gives it to us. The apostle Paul is a true example of walking in step with the Spirit to get things done. Paul, born Saul, was a highly educated and respected Jewish leader. He led a violent persecution of early Christians until he had a supernatural encounter with the risen Jesus. After his transformation, he would go on to devote his life to preaching the gospel and expanding the Christian church far and wide—traveling the breadth of the Mediterranean, from Jerusalem to Syria, Turkey, Greece, and even Rome.

Paul's personal power and abilities were not enough to get the job done. He did not teach, love, or serve others in his own strength, but he did so through the power of the Holy Spirit:

*[Christ] is the one we proclaim, admonishing and teaching everyone with all wisdom, so that we may present everyone fully mature in Christ. To this end I strenuously contend with all the energy Christ so powerfully works in me. (Colossians 1:28-29)*

God can work in supernatural ways through your life to accomplish more than you can imagine too. In his letter to the church in Ephesus, Paul acknowledges the incredible power of God, "who is able to do immeasurably more than all we ask or imagine, according to his power that is at work within us" (Ephesians 3:20). The power of God makes a difference not just for you but also for the people and places he wants to bless through you.

When Jackie Joyner-Kersee retired from track and field in 2001, she decided to return to East St. Louis to give back. Through her foundation, Joyner-Kersee has helped to make a difference in the lives of young people and families in her community and throughout the world. When asked about the key to her success, Joyner-Kersee did not hesitate: "Well, Jesus Christ, God... There's no way I could have accomplished all the things I have been blessed to do because I know it just wasn't me."[11]

You don't have to figure out how to make life happen. You don't need to bend reality or influence the universe.

You don't need to fight to overcome your weaknesses. Through Jesus, you have access to everything you need, when you need it, to become all he's created you to be.

## EMBRACING GRACE

God empowers those who follow Jesus with everything they need to accomplish everything he has planned.

## MEMORY VERSE

*But he said to me, "My grace is sufficient for you, for my power is made perfect in weakness." Therefore I will boast all the more gladly about my weaknesses, so that Christ's power may rest on me.*

*(2 Corinthians 12:9)*

# CHAPTER 7

# IDENTITY MATTERS

*"Your identity is your most valuable possession. Protect it."*[12]

**Elastigirl,** *The Incredibles*

"**W**ell, who *do* you want to be?" I posed the question to a coaching client at a decision point in her career. While she was very good at her job, she explained that work was starting to make her question herself. Whereas she had once been a team player, she had now become increasingly competitive, mistrusting, and even territorial.

"I just don't like who I am anymore," she said. "But maybe that's not actually who I am. Maybe that's just the person I need to be in order to succeed there," she continued. "I just want to be someone who knows her value, regardless of how well I do or whether people see it or not."

Later that night, I thought about the struggle we all face to define ourselves and determine our worth. We live in a performance-based culture, which can wreak havoc on our sense of self and lead us to believe we can never do enough or be good enough. Maybe that's why activist Audre Lorde once wrote, "If I don't define myself for myself, I would be crunched into other people's fantasies for me, and eaten alive."[13]

But what if the pressure we feel is not from an outside source but coming from within us? What happens when we are the ones who struggle to see the truth of who we are?

Who we are (or believe we are) has enormous implications for how we live. This question of identity drives our thoughts, feelings, and actions—and therefore our lives. So how do we find our true identity and make sure we stay on the right track?

## THE PURSUIT OF IDENTITY

The modern-day message is clear: "Be true to yourself! Be true, be you!" It's a nice-sounding thought, but what does it actually mean, and how do we achieve it?

All around us are voices clamoring to determine our identity: media and society, people we know, people we don't know, our present circumstances, and even our past. Who we are is also often what we look like, where we live, and what we do for a living. Yet, when these markers change, we're often left confused and conflicted, right back on the journey to find ourselves.

The question of identity can leave you feeling anxious and uncertain. That was me when I was beginning a new life in New York. But I was determined to figure myself out—and, as a result, find the life I was searching for. When I look back on my search for identity, I remember that there were two ideas I explored: 1) self-awareness and 2) discovering my purpose.

## 1. IN SEARCH OF SELF-AWARENESS

The philosopher Aristotle is purported to have once written, "Knowing yourself is the beginning of all wisdom." Self-awareness is about understanding what makes you a unique individual: like your thoughts and feelings, traits, motives, and tendencies. These characteristics and behaviors make up what's called your personality.

To fully explore my personality, I dove into a host of personality tests: Myers-Briggs, DISC, Enneagram, The Big 5 Personality Test, The Temperament Test, and Strengths Finder. Advocates say that these tools provide common language to communicate with others and can help us achieve a sense of belonging. Detractors, on the other hand, say that personality tests oversimplify our complex natures, and they question how reliable they actually are.

Needless to say, I was an advocate. As I read through my test results, it was like meeting myself for the first time. I felt seen and understood. Not to mention the comfort that came from knowing that there was a whole group of people just like me—assertive, analytical, and impatient. I also learned about the right environments for success and what kinds of people I would get along with best. As I kept reading, however, I started to wonder if my personality type was on someone else's avoid list, and I thought of all the people out there hoping never to get partnered with me. It wasn't a great feeling.

As I took more tests, I started choosing answers that I knew would get me a certain result: something researchers call "confirmation bias." At other times, I was answering the questions as my ideal self, curious to discover a more evolved and mature version of myself. When I agreed with the tests results, they were right. When I didn't agree, I concluded that the test was inaccurate or that I needed to take it again.

My quest for self-knowledge was starting to feel more like a curse than a blessing. Trying to explain to myself who I was, or why I was how I was, was exhausting. Besides, what did this newfound awareness mean at the end of the day?

My search for identity had brought me to another existential pursuit: one that has taken place in the hearts of people for thousands of years. No search for identity is complete without uncovering our purpose.

## 2. WHAT AM I HERE FOR?

Identity is about discovering *who* you are. Purpose is about knowing your *why*. What we believe to be our purpose will drive us. We all need a reason to get up in the morning and to keep going when challenges arise. We need to believe there is something bigger than ourselves: a brighter, better vision that makes the unknown less scary and the hardships worth enduring.

For some, their sense of purpose is connected to their vocation or work. They find great fulfillment and meaning from using their talents to achieve something significant. Others find purpose in their personal roles: as a wife, parent, or daughter. Our hobbies and interests can be another source of purpose. I read the other day about a 79-year-old woman in Miami, Florida, who had completed her lifelong dream of visiting every country in the world—193 in total. Talk about living life on purpose!

In the summer of 2017, I was determined to discover my purpose. I sought out writers and experts who had thoughts to share: Maya Angelou (*Rainbow in the Cloud*), Richard Bolles (*What Color Is Your Parachute?*), Paulo Coelho (*The Alchemist*), Viktor Frankl (*Man's Search for Meaning*), and Martha Beck (*Finding Your Own North Star*). While their perspectives were distinctive, I found alignment on some key takeaways: *be clear and intentional about what matters to you; envision clearly the life you want; trust your instincts and follow your heart; and search for what makes you truly happy.*

With each book I read, I kept having the same thought. It was all up to me! It was my responsibility to find the right path. But what if my instincts were off? What if what I thought mattered to me didn't actually make me happy? Or what if that changed? Discovering my purpose was supposed to be freeing. Yet here I was feeling daunted by the task at hand.

If purpose was about something greater than myself, then it had to connect with something or someone greater: God. I had prayed for clarity on numerous occasions, but I was still left without any concrete answers.

Turns out I was asking the wrong question. I wanted to know "Lord, what is my purpose?" The alternative question, which would shift my world, was this: "God, what is your purpose for me?"

True self-discovery comes not merely in knowing ourselves but in knowing God and what he says about us. God is not only the way to our identity and purpose; he is the source of those things because he created us. The universal search for ourselves is in fact ourselves searching for God.

## GOD'S THOUGHTS ON THE MATTER

Identity is a central concept in Christianity. In fact, to be a Christian is to have a new identity. This is how Paul puts it: "Therefore, if anyone is in Christ, the new creation has come: The old has gone, the new is here!" (2 Corinthians 5:17). Here, Paul is writing to a church experiencing social division and tensions, including favoritism based on outward appearances. Paul was instructing them—and us—to not let the world's definitions determine who we are.

In relationship with Christ, your identity is not based on what you do but based on what Jesus has done. When you put your faith in Jesus' death and resurrection, God calls you blessed and blameless—not because of your actions but because of his grace. You're now someone who is "in Christ"—you and he are inseparably joined. You're a brand new person who belongs to him.

While everything else about life will change—your job, relationships, responsibilities, finances, health and more—who you are in Christ will be the same today, tomorrow, and throughout eternity. Having a firm identity in Christ holds you steady when life's seasons and circumstances are unsteady. Knowing who you are in Christ also allows you to enjoy the brightest and best moments of life without reservation or fear of losing them, anchored in the truth of who and whose you are.

In Christ we are radically different. Jesus is not an extension of our identity—one more thing to add to a long list of identities. He becomes the determiner of who we are. The search for identity ends because we find it in him.

## A NEW IDENTITY IN CHRIST

When we accept Jesus' gift of salvation, we are freed from the world's labels, requirements, and boxes that once defined us. Because our identity is now in Christ, we can rest, knowing no amount of striving or achieving (or lack thereof) can change our identity because it's based on our faith in Jesus. You are who God says you are, not what other people believe you are—or even what you may think about yourself. What God says is the truth and what matters.

Life has a way of making you question your identity. I believe one of the pressing questions at the root of identity is whether we are enough: good enough, smart enough, attractive enough, savvy enough, interesting enough, and so on. As a result, we spend our days and years trying to measure up instead of living out the full, abundant life that Jesus has secured for us.

The reality is that in yourself *you are not enough*. You never will be. No one ever is. But because of God's grace, if you're trusting in Jesus, the following things are true of you, all the same. If ever you feel unfit or unseen, know that...

### 1. YOU ARE CHOSEN

*Even before he made the world, God loved us and chose us in Christ to be holy and without fault in his eyes.*
*(Ephesians 1:4, NLT)*

You have been on God's mind since before the beginning of time. He knew everything about you, including your flaws and faults, yet he deeply desired to know you and be known by you. God has chosen to do life with you and has a specific purpose for your life.

If ever you feel undeserving, know that...

## 2. YOU ARE LOVED

*No power in the sky above or in the earth below—
indeed, nothing in all creation will ever be able to
separate us from the love of God that is revealed in
Christ Jesus our Lord. (Romans 8:39, NLT)*

In Christ, you are loved by God, always and forever. This love is not based on your heart but based on God's heart for those who place their faith in Jesus. There is absolutely nothing you can do to cause God to love you more or less. He wants the absolute best for you and gave his Son, Jesus, so that you might have it.

If ever you feel forgotten, know that...

## 3. YOU ARE BLESSED

*All praise to God, the Father of our Lord Jesus Christ,
who has blessed us with every spiritual blessing in the
heavenly realms because we are united with Christ.
(Ephesians 1:3, NLT)*

Connected to Christ, you have God's grace and favor, which far exceeds any material blessing or goal you can achieve. God promises to protect, provide, comfort, and satisfy you—no matter what your circumstances look like. He is the source and sustainer of every good thing in your life.

If ever you feel defeated or counted out, know that...

## 4. YOU ARE VICTORIOUS

*But thanks be to God! He gives us the victory through our Lord Jesus Christ. (1 Corinthians 15:57)*

When hard times come, it can be tempting to throw in the towel. But God is in the ring with you. In fact, Jesus has already conquered sin and death. That means that you and I are free to walk into everything God has available for us, knowing that he has secured eternal treasures for us that death cannot snatch away.

### OLD SELF OFF, NEW SELF ON

Now, here's something important to know about your identity in Christ. While you are a new creation, you may not think or act like it—yet.

Imagine emigrating to a new country tomorrow. It's likely you would carry the customs and values of your original country with you. A new visa in your passport—or even a change in citizenship—wouldn't automatically change your beliefs and behaviors. But as you embraced the people and practices of your new country, in time, you would begin to walk, talk, and live differently.

The same is true of the Christian life. We are now legal citizens of God's kingdom—but learning the culture takes time.

If you are a Christian, the Bible speaks of you having a new self and an old self. The old self prioritizes your own desires and does what you think is best. The new self prioritizes God's desires and does what he says is best. The old you gives in to temptation. The new you turns away from it. The old you believes lies about God. The new you has eyes that are open to see and know the truth about God—and what he says about you and about life.

So how do we embrace the new self and let go of who we used to be? How do you become who you already are?

The Bible tells us how:

*You were taught, with regard to your former way of life, to put off your old self, which is being corrupted by its deceitful desires; to be made new in the attitude of your minds; and to put on the new self, created to be like God in true righteousness and holiness.*

*(Ephesians 4:22-24)*

Here, Paul is writing to 1st-century Christians who had received a new identity when they came to faith. Still, he needs to tell them to "put off" old-self behavior and "put on" new-self behavior. In the verses that follow, he tells them to put off falsehood and instead speak truth; to stop stealing and instead work for a living; to not speak anything unwholesome and instead use their words to build up others; to get rid of bitterness, rage and slander in their hearts and instead be kind, compassionate and forgiving (v 25-32).

But this isn't merely behavior change. This change is beyond the surface. To embrace your identity in Christ—"to put on the new self"—you have to "be made new in the attitude of your minds" (v 23). Simply put, God needs to change how you think. Unhealthy thought patterns and false beliefs can keep you stuck in your old ways.

For example, if I believe I'm running out of time to achieve a certain goal, rather than believing that God transcends time and holds mine in his hands (2 Peter

3:8), then I will likely worry and act hastily. If I believe I'm worthless rather than believing I am valuable (Matthew 6:26), then I will likely settle for less than God's best.

As Christians, we must constantly have our minds renewed by replacing the world's way of thinking with God's truth. This is not about thinking positively but thinking truthfully. One way to do that is to regularly read and study God's word (and we'll explore how to do that practically in chapter 10). But for now, consider this: what old-self attitude or behavior would you most like to "put off"? What is the new-self attitude or behavior that would replace it? And what is the truth that is going to renew your mind in the process?

## FROM WHO WE ARE TO WHY WE ARE

Understanding your true identity, who God says you are, frees you from having to prove your worth—to the world, others, or even yourself. When you know who you are in Christ, you can live with greater confidence and security. The recognition and praise of other people becomes less important. Making a great name for yourself matters less, allowing you to fulfill God's ultimate purpose for you: *to make his name great.*

We were created to glorify God, which means to bring attention to all that is admirable about him. The prophet Isaiah delivers a message from God that makes this very clear: "Bring my sons from afar and my daughters from the ends of the earth—everyone who is called by my name, whom I created for my glory, whom I formed and made" (Isaiah 43:6-7).

Throughout Scripture, we read about God's character— the things that make him great or glorious: his goodness, mercy, kindness, forgiveness, justice, wisdom, faithfulness, and so much more. We glorify God when we recognize God for who he is and respond accordingly. When we love God, trust him, obey him, and desire to please him, we give him glory. When we pray, read the Bible, thank him, and praise him, we give him glory. When we love others, forgive them, and demonstrate patience and humility, that too is glorifying God. And when we display God's glory so that other people experience him through us, and are drawn to know him and glorify him for themselves—well, then the glory multiplies!

This is the reason for our being. In fact, it is the purpose of all creation. The Bible tells us that even the skies reveal the glory of God (Psalm 19:1). I can attest! A few years back, I found myself standing on the beach in Holbox, a little island north of Mexico's Yucatán Peninsula. There, I witnessed the most majestic sunset I've ever seen. Staring past miles and miles of ocean and gazing at the sky, the only words I could gather were "My God." That is glory!

So, is that? Is that all there is to know about purpose— that we were made for God's glory? Yes and no.

Often, when people ask the "purpose" question, I think what they want to know is their unique calling or life assignment. They want to know how best to use their time, talent, and treasure to make the biggest difference or have the greatest impact.

The Bible is clear that God has certain things he wants us to do: "For we are God's handiwork, created in Christ Jesus to do good works, which God prepared in advance for us to do" (Ephesians 2:10). Just think about that for a moment: if you're a follower of Jesus,

God has prepared good things for you to do. As you begin your day, he's already gone ahead of you, lining up opportunities for you to make a positive contribution in his world.

These "good works" aren't hidden or hard to discover. The work that God finds good, that you can join him in, is serving others:

> Each of you should use whatever gift you have received to serve others, as faithful stewards of God's grace in its various forms. (1 Peter 4:10)

God gives us spiritual gifts, natural talents, and material resources to meet the needs in our homes, relationships, churches, workplaces, and communities. Wherever you are right now, I believe you have an opportunity to do good works that bring glory to God. What might he have prepared for you today?

## A RETURN TO YOUR TRUE IDENTITY

I am grateful for the many identities that shape me. I am a daughter, sister, aunt, and friend. I am an American woman of African descent. But it is my identity in Christ that is the foundation for all other identities.

As a Christian, your new identity is your true identity. Your relationship with Jesus is of greater consequence than any identity marker, role, or trait you possess. In fact, God defines you by nothing other than your faith in Jesus. United with Christ, you are chosen, blessed, loved, victorious and so much more.

The more we believe who God says we are, the more stability, security, and satisfaction we will have in this life. His word trumps what other people say—and even what we say about ourselves. He is the source of our identity and purpose. We are his children, created to know, love, and glorify him.

## EMBRACING GRACE

Through faith in Christ, you are freed from the world's labels, requirements, and boxes, which once defined you.

## MEMORY VERSE

*Therefore, if anyone is in Christ, the new creation has come: The old has gone, the new is here!*

*(2 Corinthians 5:17)*

# CHAPTER 8

# ENDLESS LOVE

*"Love is an action, never simply a feeling."*[14]

**bell hooks**

I have always loved love songs. When I was no older than six or seven, I would close my eyes and sway my head, listening to what remains one of my favorite love songs of all time: Stevie Wonder's "As." With its magnificent lyrics, composition, and arrangement, the song paints a beautiful picture of a love that will endure... until dolphins fly, the ocean covers every mountain top, and a rainbow sets the stars on fire. It's the kind of love we all hope for: *everlasting*.

Love is a universal emotion and one of the most powerful of all. Inside each of us is an unwavering desire and need for love. And while love can be hard to explain, it is also easy enough for a toddler to grasp, melting any grandparent's heart with a simple, "Wuv u."

While love is defined as a *feeling* of affection, we express love through *action*. We demonstrate love by sharing quality time, helping when there's a need, physical affection, encouragement, gifts—and in so many other ways.

Whether it's familial, friendship, or romantic, we all need to know and feel that we are loved. Love is not a small thing that we can casually regard or disregard. Our souls crave it—arguably even more than happiness, power, or purpose. Maybe that's why finding love is often as challenging as it is rewarding.

## THE PURSUIT OF LOVE

What causes love? What makes love last? What are the best ways to receive and show love? If you're looking for answers, experts offer help—proposing theories of love, components of love, love languages, and love attachment styles: all developed to help us make sense of love.

Cracking the code on love has significant health benefits. In fact, loving relationships have been linked to lower blood pressure and lower risks of heart disease.[15] Yet, building and maintaining healthy, lasting relationships is not without challenge.

Modern dating leaves many singles dazed and confused. Dating apps have increased choice but also complexity, introducing new threats and terminology to master, like ghosting (disappearing without warning) and breadcrumbing (stringing someone along).

Then there are those who marry the love of their life—only to discover that that's when the real work begins. Poor communication, lack of intimacy, boredom, stress, and money issues send formerly loved-up couples to counselors and experts to fix and figure out their marriage.

But well into my thirties, I would have given an arm and a leg to have gotten that far. I was still wishing and waiting for my "happily ever after" and was determined to do everything in my power to find it.

When I look back on my chapter of searching for love, there were two big ideas I explored: 1) be the person you want to attract and 2) you are the answer you've been waiting on.

Little did I know who I would find waiting on the other side of my search.

### 1. BE READY FOR LOVE

My older brother likes to joke that he was the better athlete in high school. He might be right; but I wasn't half bad, earning a few medals and awards from competing in track and field. As I've gotten older, I've come to appreciate even more the value of training to transform your abilities. What seems impossible in the beginning becomes achievable in the end.

There's value in preparation. As the saying goes, luck is what happens when preparation meets opportunity. Could the same be true for love?

Maybe the reason I hadn't found my "person" was because I wasn't prepared. It was time to get ready, so I got busy reading: *Loveability* (Robert Holden), *Boundaries* (Henry Cloud and John Townsend), *Attached* (Amir Levine and Rachel Heller), *All about Love* (bell hooks), and *How to Be Found by the Man You're Looking For* (Michelle McKinney Hammond).

Each of these authors spoke of the importance of being accountable in relationships and argued that we have to take responsibility for our attitudes and actions.

They all agreed that we must acknowledge and address the emotional, mental, and spiritual barriers that create challenges in our relationships. They also promoted the need to love and value oneself in order for relationships to thrive.

There was one particular idea that I remember highlighting and circling: that our struggles in relationships are generally tied to the relationship we have with ourselves. "Who you attract is a reflection of who you are," I wrote down in my journal one afternoon.

Was I attracting emotionally unavailable men because I too was emotionally unavailable? Were my personal struggles the cause of my predicament? If that was true, my only answer was to overcome every shortcoming, fault, and flaw in myself. Even with all the books, articles, and coaching programs I'd invested in, I knew that was impossible.

I didn't know what felt worse: the idea that I was destined to be alone or that somehow it was my fault. My excitement was slowly melting into a pool of despair. This was clearly not the way to love.

Instead of waiting for someone to love me, maybe I needed to take responsibility for loving myself.

## 2. BE THE LOVE YOU SEEK

"You alone are enough. You are who you've been waiting for. No matter what happens, you will always have yourself." As I wrote down each mantra, I felt the clouds parting. Here was something I could do—something completely within my own control. I could give myself the love I was looking for and quell the pressure to be chosen by another. Maybe self-love would also help me fully accept and appreciate myself. If that made me more attractive and desirable to a future mate, then that'd be great too.

After self-love affirmations, I started to actively extend kindness to myself. When I was tempted to compare myself to others, I practiced gratitude. When I started to be self-critical, I reminded myself that everyone's journey looks different. Daily journaling also helped me to speak more lovingly to myself, as I would with a friend. After a few weeks of committed self-love, I started to notice a difference.

Around that time, I also started seeing a therapist, hoping a professional could help me approach dating and relationships differently. I remember one session in particular where we were talking about lessons I had learned from past relationships.

"I need to be more understanding and less controlling," I shared. "I also need to stop putting so much pressure on myself, the guy, and the relationship."

I paused, ready to hear how self-aware and emotionally mature I was. What I heard next surprised me, to say the least.

"Do you think love will be easier if you improve yourself?" she asked.

I sat for a moment, reflecting on her question.

"I know I don't need to be perfect to be loved," I replied. "Just better than I am now," I joked.

Except she didn't laugh. She just sat there, quietly, her eyes offering care and compassion. She didn't have to say anything. I knew.

Self-love was supposed to free me from working for love. Yet here I was, still striving—just now for my own love. There was a part of me that believed I was not yet ready or worthy to be loved—by myself or by others.

It turns out that there is something far greater to experience than self-love: God's love.

## GOD'S THOUGHTS ON THE MATTER

Everlasting love is not just the stuff of love songs or fairy tales. It is a gift from God, real and available to you. The Bible tells us, "But God demonstrates his own love for us in this: While we were still sinners, Christ died for us" (Romans 5:8). God loved us well before we were faithful and loving to him. We weren't ready for or worthy of his love—nor could we ever be. Yet he pursued a loving relationship with us.

The gospel is a love story. God loves you, not in response to your love but because his nature is love. We read in the book of 1 John, "God is love" (4:8). For a long time, I was familiar with this passage of Scripture but couldn't picture what it meant exactly—until God helped me connect it to another passage of Scripture, one of the most popular and beloved in the Bible: 1 Corinthians 13:4-7.

*Love is patient, love is kind. It does not envy, it does not boast, it is not proud. It does not dishonor others, it is not self-seeking, it is not easily angered, it keeps no record of wrongs. Love does not delight in evil but rejoices with the truth. It always protects, always trusts, always hopes, always perseveres.*

Many believe that love is the greatest force in the universe. And they're right, in a way. Except that love is not a force. Love originates from a personal being.

If you're willing, would you go back and reread the previous verses and insert "God" in place of "love/ it?" Yes, right now.

Powerful, right?

This is who God is. This is how God loves.

Human love is a beautiful thing, and yet it is imperfect. Maybe love has disappointed you. Someone told you they loved you, yet they left or ended the relationship. Perhaps you're skeptical of love, unsure if you can let your guard down and allow people to love you. Or maybe you feel lonely and haven't felt loved in a very long time.

As we dig more into the truth of God's love, see if you can set aside for a moment the painful realities of human love. I believe God wants to shift things in your heart even now, if you are open to it. The love of God has transformative power—both in receiving his love and loving him in return.

## LOVED BY GOD

The message of the gospel is that God loves us. God loves you, personally. And yet, this can be a difficult truth to understand. That's why Paul prayed this prayer for a group of believers in a city called Ephesus:

> I pray that you, being rooted and established in love, may have power, together with all the Lord's holy people, to grasp how wide and long and high and deep is the love of Christ, and to know this love that surpasses knowledge—that you may be filled to the measure of all the fullness of God. (Ephesians 3:17-19)

As expansive as our galaxy is, we can measure its mass. As large as an ocean is, we can measure its depth. As tall as the tallest mountain is, we can measure its height. But God's love cannot be measured—it "surpasses knowledge." It is limitless. His love will never run out, and he will never change his mind about loving you. That means you can share whatever is on your heart, openly and honestly. You can ask him for what you need. And you can trust that he will be with you through thick and thin.

As Paul prays, we can be "rooted and established" in God's love (v 17). When I think about the word "rooted," I picture the beautiful magnolia trees we have in North and South Carolina. Some can grow to be 40ft wide, with roots as deep as their width. A tree with deep roots is secure in extreme weather, such as hurricanes, which we also get from time to time. Like these beautiful trees, you and I can withstand the storms of life when we're rooted in the safety of God's love.

It's tempting to believe we can love ourselves to wholeness: that, with enough attention and care, we can find confidence, security, and rest within ourselves. That's what I was looking for through all the positive affirmations and journal entries and books I read. The reality is that I'm just not that powerful. Neither are you. Nor is there a romantic partner out there—or any human—who can make you whole. But God can.

Read again what Paul prays for the Ephesians: "... that you may be filled to the measure of all the fullness of God" (v 19). The New Living Translation puts it like this: "Then you will be *made complete* with all the fullness of life and power that comes from God" (emphasis added). The "fullness of God" is everything that God is: his nature, characteristics, attributes, and so on. Having a deeper revelation of God's love can help you grow spiritually and make important changes in your life. You can become better at navigating a tense relationship, for example. Or you find the strength and motivation to improve your financial situation or your relationship with food. God's love strengthens, satisfies, and transforms us.

We can't complete ourselves. Nor can anyone else complete us, no matter what the movies say. But God's love makes us whole.

## THE GREATEST COMMANDMENT

God loves you. The other side of the coin is that we are to love God. This is the first and greatest commandment that Jesus gives: "Love the Lord your God with all your heart and with all your soul and with all your mind" (Matthew 22:37). This love is not based solely on feelings or emotions, but it is a decision to trust and commit fully to God and what he wants for our lives, above our own plans and desires.

We are to love God with everything we have, not because God needs our love but because his love is good for us. Let me explain. When someone has your heart, they have a great influence on you—your thoughts, feelings, and decisions, and even your identity. That also means that our hearts are at risk of things like disappointment, hurt, and rejection.

But loving God first and most protects our hearts. We find hope and fulfillment in him, not in other people, who may try to be our "everything" but cannot be. Our hearts are rooted in God: someone who does not change, has no conflicting interests, and who wants nothing but the best for us at all times. He becomes and remains the one who has the greatest influence on us—an influence that is for good and never for ill.

When we love God as he intends us to, we are also able to fulfill the second most important command that Jesus gives: *to love others* (v 39).

The Bible tells us that loving God means we must love people (1 John 4:21). The love we give flows out of the love we receive. Because God's love never runs out, we are able to love more deeply and freely—without fear or obligation, or needing anything in return. We can love even when we don't feel like it or feel like we have nothing left to give.

Our acts of love toward others are a visible demonstration of our invisible God.

It's why the apostle John wrote, "No one has ever seen God; but if we love one another, God lives in us and his love is made complete in us" (v 12). Another translation says his love is "brought to full expression in us" (NLT). As believers, we are commanded to love people as God loves us.

## EXPERIENCING TRUE LOVE

Many of us believe God loves us. Yet this truth is more of an intellectual understanding than experiential knowledge. There can be a disconnect between *knowing* God's love and *feeling* his love. While God's love is a fact, his love can also be felt. The Bible tells us that the Holy Spirit pours out his love into our hearts (Romans 5:5). The following are ways in which we can seek God and enter into his loving presence.

## 1. PRAISE HIM

We praise people all the time: through compliments, kudos, and commendations. More than people, God is worthy of our praise: for his love, faithfulness, provision, protection, kindness, and so much more. Praise reminds us of our dependency on God and how blessed we are to have him in our lives through Jesus. When we praise God, he will warm our hearts towards him, and he'll remind us of his care for us.

Music is a great way of praising God—so put together a playlist of all your favorites and make time to sing along. Or if running or dance is your thing, turn on the music and get going! Or commit to telling someone at church on Sunday one thing you're praising the Lord for from your week. The possibilities for praising God are as endless as he is!

> Praise the LORD. How good it is to sing praises to our God, how pleasant and fitting to praise him!
>
> (Psalm 147:1)

## 2. ENJOY HIS CREATION

Have you ever gotten a gift from someone and felt their love? Gifts are a physical representation of the fact that we are known and appreciated. If you've ever felt sentimental when walking in the park or sitting surrounded by nature, consider this: you are experiencing a divine gift from God. God created nature to reveal who he is—and we have the privilege of enjoying this gift.

Think about how you can experience nature throughout your day: maybe that could be a few moments in the morning spent looking out of the window at the sky, or a short walk at lunchtime, or stepping outside after dinner to look at the stars. Receive these gifts and remember that you're loved.

> Look at the birds of the air; they do not sow or reap or store away in barns, and yet your heavenly Father feeds them. Are you not much more valuable than they? (Matthew 6:26)

### 3. LOVE OTHERS

If we are going to love people with the love of God, we need God to fill our hearts with his love. This is what God does for his people through Jesus. But one way we often *feel* more of God's love is when we love others; as we pour love out to other people, he pours love into us. As we've seen in the second greatest commandment, we are called to love our neighbors—that is, any and everyone who crosses our path. At the same time, the passages on love that we find in the New Testament of the Bible are actually addressing church communities: our church family are the people who are meant to be *especially* dear to us.

So, if you are a Christian, do you belong to a church? If the answer to that question is no, you'll find some guidance on finding a church later on in chapter 10. Or if you *do* already go to a church, do you *know* people there? Do you *love* people there? Do you invest as much time and energy in those relationships as you do trying to secure a date? How could you seek not only to receive from your church family but also to love (and give) generously?

*My command is this: Love each other as I have loved*
*you. (John 15:12)*

## 4. BE LOVED BY OTHERS

God wants us to experience his amazing love not only
from him directly but also from the people around
us. We all need personal relationships where we feel a
sense of closeness and belonging. But for some of us,
allowing people to love us is difficult. We would prefer
not to ask for help or let others see our vulnerabilities.
But God wants us to freely and gratefully accept his
love demonstrated through other people.

Again, God's primary vehicle for this is the local
church. God's people are the body of Christ: his hands,
feet, and shoulders, so to speak. They are there—we
are here—to lend a helping hand, walk through a new
season with you, and offer you a shoulder to help you
carry a heavy load. What would it look like to open
yourself up to receiving the love of your spiritual
family?

*Be devoted to one another in love. Honor one another*
*above yourselves. (Romans 12:10)*

## A BEAUTIFUL PICTURE OF GOD'S LOVE

The parable of the Lost Son is one of Jesus' most
famous stories (Luke 15:11-32). As Jesus tells it, there
once was a man who had two sons. The younger son
asked his father for his share of the inheritance. Soon
after receiving it, the son left home and settled in a
distant country. He lived recklessly, squandered all his

money, and ended up destitute and alone. Regretful and ashamed, he decided to return home.

The older son, on the other hand, dutifully served their father while his brother was away, following all the rules and being a model citizen. He did all the right things while his brother chose to do the very opposite.

Can you imagine how the younger son must have felt, returning home after all those years? Having to face his father and brother, hungry, dirty, and with no one to blame but himself. As the son neared home, he saw a figure in the distance approaching him—perhaps a lost traveler or one of his father's servants. But as he continued to walk, he realized that the person running towards him was none other than his father! When the two finally met, his father threw his arms around the son and kissed him.

Broken and full of grief, the son declared, "Father, I have sinned against heaven and against you. I am no longer worthy to be called your son" (v 21). But his father, overcome with great joy, called for a party to be thrown in honor of his son returning home.

If the son was in disbelief, so was his older brother. In fact, he refused to join the celebration. He was the one who had faithfully served their father all those years. Yet, his little brother had left, broken all the rules, crawled back home, and got the red-carpet treatment.

So the father went out to the older son too—despite his rude and spiteful refusal to come to the party. The parable ends with the father's words to his elder son:

*You are always with me, and everything I have is yours. But we had to celebrate and be glad, because*

*this brother of yours was dead and is alive again; he
was lost and is found. (v 31-32)*

## LOST AND FOUND

Before returning home, the lost son was feeding pigs
when he realized that they were eating better than he
was. Talk about rock bottom! That was when, as the
Scripture puts it, "He came to his senses" (v 17).

Maybe you can relate?

Perhaps you've had an epiphany about yourself or your
life when you realized, "This is not me," or wondered
how you had ended up in a far-off place. Perhaps you're
going through something right now which has led you
to this book. No matter where you've been or what
you've done, God is waiting for you.

Or maybe you can relate to the older brother. You
have been doing all the right things and have been a
"good" Christian, and yet everyone seems to be enjoying
the things you have yet to experience. Or maybe you
have what you prayed for, but the reality is far from
what you had hoped. You may feel resentment or
disappointment. God is waiting for you too.

We all get lost in different ways. Whether you're lost
in the world, lost in rules, or lost in yourself, I want you
to know that God is running towards you with open
arms. You have a heavenly Father who loves you and
who has shown you, in sending Jesus to save you, how
much he wants you to be part of his family.

In all your searching, he has been searching for you
too.

## EMBRACING GRACE

God's love strengthens, satisfies, and transforms us.

## MEMORY VERSE

*This is how God showed his love among us: He sent his one and only Son into the world that we might live through him. (1 John 4:9)*

PART THREE

# Surrendering

# CHAPTER 9

# LET GO

*"The moment of surrender is not when life is over.
It's when it begins."*[16]

**Marianne Williamson**

The month of March in New York is supposed to mark the end of winter, although an inch or two of snow is not uncommon. While April ushers in the spring, a time of new beginnings, March can feel like a flight delay that keeps getting longer and longer. That was me in 2018, waiting for life to warm up and reawaken something inside of me.

I had dedicated nearly four years to improving myself and my life. I had pursued happiness, only to realize I couldn't sustain it. My search for power had revealed that I wasn't strong enough. Trying to find myself, I had wound up getting lost in myself. And looking for love had showed me that I could not satisfy the longings in my heart.

I couldn't fix, figure out, or find what I was looking for. The more I tried to, the less satisfied I became. Self-help had made big promises but failed to deliver.

One chilly Sunday morning, I was all out of ideas. I didn't want to read any more self-help books, plans, strategies, or theories. I knew I'd feel good initially, excited about the opportunity to learn and grow. But experience had taught me that any change would be short-lived or fall short.

Sometimes, the truth can be right in front of us and we don't see it. Until one day, we do.

I didn't need self-help. I needed the Savior's help.

Striving was not the solution; surrender was.

I had come to the end of myself. And when I got there, Jesus was waiting.

## THE POWER OF SURRENDER

*Surrender.* It can be a tough idea to appreciate, conjuring up images of battle, the threat of capture, or even death. Surrendering signals that you are outmatched and about to lose. You have no choice but to give up. So you place your life in the hands of an adversary, fearing punishment and with little hope for a brighter future.

Biblical surrender, on the other hand, is an act of faith, not fear. We freely give up control of our lives and trust that God, who loves us, wants the best for us. We recognize his ultimate authority over everything he created, including ourselves.

Scripture is full of examples of surrender, and, as always, Jesus is the clearest model for us. In everything Jesus did, he submitted himself to his Father's plan. Teaching in the synagogue in Capernaum, he declared his intention: "For I have come down from heaven not to do my will but to do the will of him who sent me" (John 6:38).

We also see a vivid picture of surrender in the Garden of Gethsemane, where Jesus, facing death, prayed that God's will would be done and not his own (Luke 22:42). Jesus knew God's purpose for his life and death, but that didn't make his assignment easy.

So Jesus is someone who understands that surrender doesn't always feel good or look pretty. Yet the difficulty of surrendering pales in comparison with what we gain. When we willingly give up our lives, we experience the abundant life that God desires we have. Let me say that again. When we willingly give up our lives, we experience the abundant life that God desires we have. Here are the words of Jesus himself:

> Then Jesus said to his disciples, "Whoever wants to be my disciple must deny themselves and take up their cross and follow me. For whoever wants to save their life will lose it, but whoever loses their life for me will find it." (Matthew 16:24-25)

At this point in his ministry, Jesus is riding a wave of popularity. Great crowds are coming to listen to him, and his disciples are right there, in the middle of the action. It must have felt pretty good! But in the verses just before these ones, Jesus reveals to his disciples what his mission will ultimately involve: his brutal death and miraculous resurrection (v 21). As if that wasn't shocking enough, he then tells them that if anyone wants to be his follower, they too must be willing to give up their life. He even uses the metaphor of a crucifixion, possibly the worst way to die in that day. Jesus wanted his point to be clear: surrender is a serious matter. And it's an unavoidable part of being his disciple.

Let's examine this verse more closely to understand what Jesus is saying about surrender. As you reflect, consider what this might look like for you:

- **Deny yourself.** We must turn away from ourselves and what displeases or dishonors God. The natural self is wired to prioritize our desires, pleasures, and satisfaction above God. When we deny ourselves, we let go of trying to get everything we can out of this life or have things our way.

- **Take up your cross.** To remain faithful to Christ, we must be willing to make sacrifices in this world. That might mean our ambitions, reputation, relationships, and comforts. We must lay aside our pride and humble ourselves to follow Christ.

- **Follow me.** When we follow Jesus, we pattern our lives after him. We love him and value him above anyone and anything else. We obey his teachings and allow him to guide our lives as he sees fit. He becomes our primary pursuit.

If you want the new life Jesus has for you, you will have to give up your old life. When you try to hold on to your old way of life, it's at the expense of your soul and your relationship with Jesus. But when you surrender your life and let Jesus take center stage—when you deny yourself, take up your cross, and follow him—then, paradoxically, you find your life. You get to enjoy a life with Christ, finding real peace and satisfaction in him in this life. And you have the assurance that your soul is secure with him in the next.

Here's something important I want you to consider.

Your new self and your new life, which comes from surrender, will be unique to you. I used to think I would have to look and act a certain way to follow Jesus: that I wouldn't be able to be "myself" or enjoy life. This is a lie. The truth is that who you are in Christ is the real you, and following Jesus is *how* you live fully and freely. God knows exactly what he's placed inside of you, what he's planned for you, and what he will prepare you to do.

Still, I want to be clear. Giving up your life is not a natural thing to do. Because of sin, we are wired to hold on to control... and to ourselves! Therefore, surrender is a supernatural act of God. We give him a heart that is willing to be made willing. He gives us power and ability. You don't have to figure out how to surrender. God only needs your desire to begin. Is that you? Could you ask him to help you to take the next step?

When we surrender, we allow Jesus to reign in our hearts. His rule as King over our lives is what it means to be a Christian. And when we embrace Jesus as our King, we're invited to become part of what he is doing in the world, as citizens of the kingdom of God.

## A NEW WAY OF LIVING

There is an alternate reality from the one you see: one that runs counter to the world's wisdom and values. Here, every detail of your life serves a greater good. No circumstance or experience is ever wasted. In this reality, God is transforming his people, and the earth, into everything he intends us to be. If you have placed your faith in Jesus, you are part of this alternative realm, known as the kingdom of God.

*Once, on being asked by the Pharisees when the kingdom of God would come, Jesus replied, "The coming of the kingdom of God is not something that can be observed, nor will people say, 'Here it is,' or 'There it is,' because the kingdom of God is in your midst." (Luke 17:20-21)*

Jesus' ministry was devoted to teaching about the kingdom of God: the rule and reign of God in heaven and on earth. The Jewish religious leaders, known as Pharisees, believed that the kingdom of God was a future state when their nation, Israel, would return to political prominence. They were waiting for God to send them a powerful king to wage war against the Roman Empire and other foreign oppressors.

Jesus, however, told them that God's rule had come. The King of the kingdom was standing right in front of them.

You see, they were looking for the kingdom with their physical eyes. But Jesus was emphasizing the inward aspect of the kingdom, where God rules in the hearts of his people, not just in the physical world. Through his life, death, and resurrection, Jesus makes it possible for us to enter the kingdom of God by faith, and to surrender our lives to him.

Today, Christians are citizens of God's kingdom while living on earth. That means we face two fundamentally different and competing realities. The central difference might be summed up like this: *Love, trust, and live for God*: the kingdom of God. Or *love, trust, and live for yourself*: the kingdom of the world. Both kingdoms ask for our allegiance; but, ultimately, we have to choose. On the surface, the kingdom of the world promises much—yet if we consider things closely, we'll see that true peace, security, or freedom can only be found in God.

1. **The world says:** *You must do everything you can to meet your needs.* **The kingdom of God says:** *God's got you.* Jesus' death and resurrection have already supplied your greatest spiritual needs for forgiveness and new life. Having provided that, he's not going to let you down with the smaller things either, like a job or somewhere to live, or people to love. And if you ever do find yourself in a season of lack or difficulty, you can know that through it, God is working to meet some other, deeper need in you that will only be for your good.

   *And my God will meet all your needs according to the riches of his glory in Christ Jesus. (Philippians 4:19)*

2. **The world says:** *It's up to you to determine where you go in life.* **The kingdom of God says:** *God will give you direction.* Through faith in Jesus, God turns your life around and sets you on a path to eternity with him. And he's going to guide your every step between now and then, to make sure you get there. You don't have to plan for every scenario or perfect every step because you have Jesus on the journey.

   *Trust in the LORD with all your heart and lean not on your own understanding; in all your ways submit to him, and he will make your paths straight. (Proverbs 3:5-6)*

3. **The world says: *You are responsible for your own happiness*. The kingdom of God says: *God will give you joy*.** The joy of the Lord is in the spirit of every believer. This kind of happiness is not contingent on everything going right or the way you desire. It is not based on *what* is going on but on *who* is with you through it all. Even in difficult circumstances, you can rejoice, knowing that God loves you and will never leave you alone.

*You make known to me the path of life; you will fill me with joy in your presence, with eternal pleasures at your right hand. (Psalm 16:11)*

4. **The world says: *You have to look out for yourself*. The kingdom of God says: *God will fight your battles*.** Everywhere we turn, there seems to be conflict and chaos waiting to threaten our well-being and livelihood. The challenges feel like more than we can handle. But those who trust in Jesus have the Holy Spirit to shield us from harm and keep us in his loving protection. God will deal with your enemies; you don't have to take matters into your own hands.

*Be strong in the Lord and in his mighty power. Put on the full armor of God, so that you can take your stand against the devil's schemes.*

*(Ephesians 6:10-11)*

5. **The world says: *There's no time to rest*. The kingdom of God says: *God will give you rest*.** Keeping up with the world's expectations (and our own) is a full-time job. Striving to be chosen, loved,

or good enough is a heavy burden to bear. But in Christ, you have the assurance that you are made right with God not through your own efforts but by placing your faith in Jesus. You cannot do it all—and you don't have to.

*Come to me, all you who are weary and burdened, and I will give you rest. (Matthew 11:28)*

I believe the change you are looking for—what your soul is searching for—is found in the kingdom of God. We enter this new way of life by ceasing our striving and instead surrendering to Jesus as King and embracing his rule. Through surrender, we find the path to everything God intends for us.

## THE PATH OF LIFE

In his final days, Jesus and his disciples shared a meal together, known as the Last Supper, in the city of Jerusalem. During their time together, Jesus told them not to be troubled. He assured them that he was going away to prepare a place in his "Father's house" for them and that he would return. Jesus was talking about heaven, but one of his disciples, Thomas, was confused:

*Lord, we don't know where you are going, so how can we know the way? (John 14:5).*

Thomas was trying to figure out how to get to the place Jesus was promising.

When it comes to navigating life, often we focus on the *how*. What method or strategy will get us from point A to point B? What is the way, we ask ourselves?

For the Christian, however, the answer is not *how* but *who*. Jesus is the way. In response to Thomas's question, Jesus replied:

*I am the way and the truth and the life. No one comes to the Father except through me. (v 6)*

You don't have to navigate different and endless routes to get to the life you're looking for. You can ditch the how-to, put your hand into Jesus' hand, and let him take you there.

*Jesus is the way:* he is the path to the life God has called you to live.

*Jesus is the truth:* he frees you from every lie that separates you from God.

*Jesus is the life:* he is the source of abundant and everlasting life.

You have the opportunity to give back to Jesus the life he gave you. You get to trade in exhaustive pursuits for a single aim. This one thing, the most important thing, takes care of all the other things you need most in life.

## EMBRACING GRACE
When we willingly give up our lives, we experience the abundant life that God desires we have.

## MEMORY VERSE

*For whoever wants to save their life will lose it, but whoever loses their life for me will find it.*

*(Matthew 16:25)*

CHAPTER 10

# SEEK FIRST

*"It's time for you to move, realizing that the thing you are seeking is also seeking you."* [17]

Iyanla Vanzant

We all are in pursuit of something. We devote significant time and energy to making money, advancing in our careers, being a good spouse or parent, working out, eating well, and so much more. Recognizing we need help, we consume copious amounts of information, advice, and guidance in hopes of obtaining what we seek.

But no one seeks God. None of us.

That's not my opinion or judgement. I'm simply sharing what the Bible says:

*There is no one righteous, not even one; there is no one who understands; there is no one who seeks God.*
(Romans 3:10-11)

Here, the apostle Paul is telling us the fundamental truth of our human condition. We may seek things that God can give us—joy, peace, satisfaction, and fulfillment, for instance. But no one naturally seeks God until the Holy Spirit changes the condition of their heart. We cannot search for God or find God unless he seeks us.

This was Jesus' very mission on earth:

*For the Son of Man came to seek and to save the lost.*
*(Luke 19:10)*

God sent Jesus to search for those separated from him. Once found, we are to surrender to Jesus. As we let go of our lives, we take up a new pursuit. As Christians, we are called to seek the kingdom of God.

## FIRST THINGS FIRST

During his famous Sermon on the Mount, Jesus shares a vision of a whole new way of life. In the second half of the sermon, he calls the people listening not to worry about the everyday concerns of life: what to eat or drink or what clothes to wear (Matthew 6:25). He then tells them where instead to put their energy and attention.

*But seek first his kingdom and his righteousness, and*
*all these things will be given to you as well. (v 33)*

Jesus is saying that when we pursue God's kingdom first, he will take care of everything else. To seek God's kingdom and his righteousness means our very first concern is living as God would have us live. It's about aligning ourselves and our lives with what his word says. It means exercising humility, patience, and gentleness, for example. It means acting lovingly towards people, even when they treat us differently. It means delighting ourselves in what pleases God above what is pleasing to us.

So, what about our other pursuits? Is Jesus saying we should not care about our livelihoods or how we will survive? Certainly not. Elsewhere in the Bible, for example, God calls Christians who are able to work to do so, so that they can eat (2 Thessalonians 3:12). But what Jesus *is* saying is that we don't need to *worry* about these things. He is promising that your Father in heaven will take care of you when you put him first. When you do that, God promises to provide for your needs in the way he determines is best (even if it's not what we'd expect or ask for). It is no longer all up to you. You are not on your own.

The question is: Do you believe that God will fulfill his promise? Are you confident that God will help you and take care of you? Are you willing to stop chasing the things of this world and instead give yourself to seeking the things of God's kingdom?

At the heart of surrender and seeking God's kingdom is the matter of faith. Fundamentally, we cannot trust God or even have a relationship with him without it. If you only know one thing about faith, please know this: faith does not come from ourselves. It is a gift from God produced by the Holy Spirit. Yet, God grows our faith through various practices he's given us—not ends in themselves but the means by which we stay connected to God and seek his kingdom.

Let's devote a little time to examining three of the most important habits of faith we can build: *Bible reading, prayer, and church community.* I encourage you to approach each one with fresh eyes and an open heart—whether you're a new believer, curious about Christianity, or strengthening your walk with Christ.

## THE BOOK OF ALL BOOKS

If you are searching for answers to life's biggest questions, there's a book for that. There are thousands and thousands, in fact. However, there is one book that separates itself from the pack—the most read, most widely distributed, and best-selling book of all time: the Holy Bible.

Packed with historical records and accounts, letters, songs, and more, the Bible has 66 books in total, divided into two main sections: the Old Testament (39 books) and the New Testament (27 books). The Bible starts with an account of God's creation of the world and ends with God's promise to live with his people for all of eternity. The life of Jesus is detailed in the first four books of the New Testament, known as the Gospels.

Yet the Bible is not just a book *about* God. Rather, Christians believe the Bible is the holy word *of* God: his message to humanity through human authors. The word of God is powerful. God spoke, and creation came into being. Jesus, who is called the Word of God, spoke, and souls were set free. The written word of God, the Bible, also has tremendous power:

*For the word of God is alive and active. Sharper than any double-edged sword, it penetrates even to dividing soul and spirit, joints and marrow; it judges the thoughts and attitudes of the heart. (Hebrews 4:12)*

God's word can help us battle lies and unhealthy thoughts that attack our faith and impede our walk with God.

Throughout the pages of Scripture, we also learn about God's character and his nature. For example, we read about his faithfulness and divine providence in the story of Joseph. We see God at work in our everyday activities from the story of Ruth. From the story of Esther, we see that even when God seems absent, he's working on our behalf. And all those stories foreshadow and point forward to the main event: the life, death, and resurrection of Jesus. He is the one who reveals God's character most clearly.

The Bible is a diverse book with varying types of literature. But whether we're reading stories, poetry, letters, or prophetic warnings, there is so much treasure for us to gather: "The Holy Scriptures ... are able to make you wise for salvation through faith in Jesus Christ" (2 Timothy 3:15), and "everything that was written in the past was written to teach us, so that through the endurance taught in the Scriptures and the encouragement they provide we might have hope" (Romans 15:4).

Now, there may be parts of Scripture that seem implausible or frankly irrelevant. You will likely have questions, even misgivings, as you read. Countless scholars devote their entire lives to unraveling the mysteries of Scripture, and they struggle too! Please don't let that prevent you from hearing God speak through his word. Getting to know God is the journey of a lifetime—but it's a journey you can start today.

Here are some things to consider as you get started or keep going with reading the Bible:

- **Make a plan to read the Bible.** It's amazing the

things we do when they're on our calendars. Pick a specific time each day to read the word and stick to it. It doesn't have to be a lot of time; try 15 minutes and adjust as necessary.

- **Pick a book of the Bible and read a little portion every day.** This can help you better understand what the verses mean in their context. You can absolutely read the Bible straight through starting in Genesis. But if you're new to the Bible, I would recommend the Gospels: Matthew, Mark, Luke, and John.

- **Pray and ask God to help you.** Understanding the Bible is not a feat of academic intelligence. There's something spiritual going on. So we need to ask God to help us understand his word. He will give us clarity and revelation when we ask.

- **Read... slowly!** Read it once. Read it a second time. Listen to an audio Bible if that helps. Take your time as you read, recognizing that the Bible is God's word. What a blessed to hear from and communicate with God!

- **Interact with the text.** You could start by asking yourself the following: 1) What does this tell me about God? 2) What does this tell me about people? 3) How can I apply this to my own life as a follower of Jesus? You could also use a devotional resource to guide you through. There are some suggestions for this (and everything else in this chapter) at the back of the book.

- **Continue to pray.** Talk to God about what you've read. Pray that he would water the seeds of Scripture planted and that his word will help inform your daily living.

Reading the Bible will help you gain confidence in and assurance of what you believe. God's desire is that you mature spiritually, growing in truth and understanding. He wants you to overcome temptation, sin, and anything else holding you back from the life he intends for you. Perhaps most amazing of all, when you open the Bible, God promises to speak to you and show you himself. That is an amazing privilege.

But it's not the only one. Not only has God given us his word to live by faith; he has also given us the miraculous gift of prayer.

### PRAYER: A DIRECT LINE TO GOD

Martin Luther King is quoted as saying, "To be a Christian without prayer is no more possible than to be alive without breathing." The Bible is clear: "Pray continually" (1 Thessalonians 5:17). You see, prayer is not merely a formal act but communication with God. It is our direct line to heaven.

Yet prayer isn't merely a monologue; it is dynamic communion with the living God, who hears us—and who responds. It is through this communion that we are strengthened to live by faith. We are able to express to God our gratitude and acknowledge his goodness. We recognize the Spirit leading and guiding us along our path. Through prayer, we experience God's comfort and peace during difficult circumstances.

Prayer is also a time to confidently ask God for what we need (Hebrews 4:16).

It is also through prayer that God's will is done on earth through our lives. How does God mend, restore, and heal people and the world he created? He does it through us. How do we join him in what he's doing? When we pray for his will to be done and for our hearts and hands to be committed to the work.

Jesus knew prayer was so important that he took time to teach his disciples how to pray. You may know the Lord's Prayer, found in the books of Luke and Matthew. This prayer is a reminder that praying is more than asking God for what we want and need. Our priority is that God's will be done.

Let's walk through the Lord's Prayer and examine how it can influence our prayer life. Let each line serve as a starting point as you speak to God in your own words too.

- **Our Father in heaven, hallowed be your name.** Talk to God about how holy, sacred, and good he is. Take a moment to be still and revere God, the creator and sustainer of all life. Acknowledge that he is perfect and you are not. Allow that truth to soften your heart as you seek him in this moment of prayer.

- **Your kingdom come, your will be done, on earth as in heaven.** Share with God your desire for his will to be done, not your own. If this feels hard for you, be honest with him—and ask that he would help you to prioritize his kingdom. You might also acknowledge and surrender any desires you're holding tightly to, letting God know that you trust him to do what is best.

- **Give us today our daily bread.** This is the time to ask God for what you need today. Focusing your requests on the present moment helps you release the fear and anxiety of what the future holds. God is present when you pray and will provide for your daily needs.

- **Forgive us our sins as we forgive those who sin against us.** Confess your sin to God: bring to mind any ways in which you've fallen short in the last day or week and say sorry to the Lord. Then talk to him about anyone who has wronged or angered you; ask God to help you to forgive them.

- **Lead us not into temptation but deliver us from evil.** Pray that God would protect your heart and mind from the temptations you face. Admit your weaknesses and ask for his strength to keep you on the right path. If you are in a bind, ask God to show you how to get out of the situation. Thank God for sending Jesus to carry you through all trials.

- **For the kingdom, the power, and the glory are yours now and forever.** Declare that God reigns over all creation and overrides all other powers and authorities. Bring to mind ways in which God has demonstrated his power in your life and in the lives of others. Praise him for who he is: holy, wise, loving, compassionate, mighty, and so much more.

• **Amen.** Ask God that everything you've prayed be according to his will. Know that he hears you because of Jesus and the relationship with God that he makes possible.

## GATHERING TOGETHER

When it comes to making changes in our lives, it can be tempting to forge ahead alone. They don't call it "self-help" for nothing! But no woman or man is an island. We need other people to help us grow. For the Christian, this rings all the truer. Like Bible reading and prayer, being part of a church community enables us to strengthen our faith, stay on the right path, and become the people God wants us to be. (And listening to God and speaking to God are two important things that Christians do together when they meet.)

The Bible is clear that being a solo Christian is not God's desire for us. In fact, when we unite with Jesus, we unite with every believer worldwide to form the body of Christ:

> For just as each of us has one body with many members,
> and these members do not all have the same function,
> so in Christ we, though many, form one body, and each
> member belongs to all the others. (Romans 12:4-5)

God has given each of us specific attributes, skills, and gifts to strengthen, build, comfort, and challenge one another. Just as the arm serves the hand or the hip supports the leg, so we as believers are connected to each other and are to serve one another. If you're a believer, you're an important part of this body; some other body part is counting on you!

That means we're going to need to *gather* as a church, meeting regularly with Christians near us: "Let us not neglect our meeting together, as some people do, but encourage one another, especially now that the day of [Jesus'] return is drawing near" (Hebrews 10:25, NLT). When we gather to worship God, read Scripture, take communion, pray, and hear his word preached, we find help to live out the faith we believe. We are motivated to keep loving and doing good, to not abandon Christ during difficult times but to remain connected to one another and to Jesus.

After four years of living in New York, God directed me to Washington, D.C., where I found a wonderful church home. Being in a church community has led to profound changes in my life. I have experienced God's love, healing, and faithfulness in relationships with cherished sisters and brothers in Christ. I have been uplifted, instructed, and compelled to live in alignment with the truth of God. I've also been blessed to encourage and support others.

Now, that's not to say that church fellowship is always easy. Joining a new church and connecting with people who likely have strong, established relationships takes time and patience. Navigating a church's unique dynamics can be puzzling. Feeling shy and awkward is completely normal. Or it may be that you have been let down by people within the church in the past. This hurt may have caused you to give up on going or even distorted your view of God.

If you connect with any of this, my prayer is that God will meet you at your place of need and stir within you a desire to find a church home. There are genuine, warm, grace-filled people who would love to walk alongside you as you pursue Jesus and grow in your relationship with God.

There is no perfect church, but we do have a perfect Savior. He is devoted to his church and to placing you in community to be blessed and be a blessing to others.

Whether you're a new Christian, new to town, or desiring to grow in your faith, here are some tips for joining a church community:

1. **Pray.** Ask God to guide your search for a church home and to help you make a commitment once you've found one. Pray for the courage, humility, and patience needed along the journey.

2. **Determine your needs and preferences.** A church that preaches the truth from the Bible is a need. Then there are preferences: a church that is large or small, new or established, casual or formal. These are fine to have too, but don't compromise on your needs in pursuit of your preferences. Gaining clarity on what's important to you will help you with the next step.

3. **Research.** Go online and search for churches in your local area. Check out their websites or social media to learn more. And don't forget to ask friends, family, and colleagues for recommendations.

4. **Visit.** Make a short list of churches and make a plan to start visiting. You may have to visit a couple of different churches, and you may need to go several times before you decide. But it's best not to spend too long in limbo. (Depending on

where you live, there might be a different church for every week of the year!)

5. **Keep praying.** Ask God to help you narrow down your church choices and make it clear when you have found your home—while recognizing that it may take time to feel part of the family.

6. **Get involved and engaged.** Once you join a church, go all-in, as much as you're able; commit to being there each Sunday, join a ministry or small group, participate in Bible study, pray corporately, and serve. It's as you engage that you'll feel a sense of belonging and strengthen the foundation of your faith.

## LIFE MORE ABUNDANTLY

The New Testament instructs Jesus' earliest disciples to regularly pray, hear the word, gather for worship, and more. God knew they would need a strong spiritual foundation and resilient faith for the mission ahead. In the same way, these practices help deepen our connection with Jesus and allow us to live the life he has called us to: an *abundant* life. Jesus said:

*The thief comes only to steal and kill and destroy; I have come that they may have life, and have it to the full. (John 10:10)*

Here, Jesus is talking to a group of religious leaders about his ministry. The leaders, called Pharisees, insisted on perfect behavior in order to be right with God. This was not only impossible, but it also created a heavy burden for people. Jesus called them thieves because they were robbing people of the truth and the life it brings.

On the other hand, Jesus was there to bring life to the people. And not just life but *life to the full*. It's a picture of abundance. This is not about material prosperity or success but something greater.

Abundant life is a life free from striving to be good enough, do enough, or have enough. A life where there is joy, peace, and satisfaction—not due to our external circumstances but due to our satisfied souls. It is a secure life, knowing you are connected to the primary source of everything you need.

Jesus came to give us new life, abundant life, and eternal life. Our response is to surrender and seek him. In doing so, we find everything we've been searching for.

## EMBRACING GRACE
When we pursue God's kingdom first, he will take care of everything else.

## MEMORY VERSE

*But seek first his kingdom and his righteousness, and all these things will be given to you as well.*
(Matthew 6:33)

# WHERE NEXT?

When I turned from self-help and back to Jesus, I had no idea of the fresh start God had in store. In June 2018, I left New York and relocated to Washington, D.C., where I joined Grace Covenant Church. Over the next three years, I got to know Jesus—and myself too—in new and profound ways through this incredible community. I built relationships there that I am forever grateful to have had. Then, in 2022, given work flexibility and a desire to be closer to my family, I relocated to Charlotte, NC. Soon after, I found a home at The Park Church, where I get to help new members and those new to the faith connect and grow.

Since ditching the how-to life, I have experienced new levels of joy, satisfaction, security, and purpose through the daily decision to let go, seek God's kingdom, and embrace grace. It hasn't always been easy or comfortable, but it's been necessary to walk more fully into who God has called me to be. And while my self-help-obsessed days are over, I can't help but imagine what new chapters and changes await, as God continues to work in, around, and through me.

Well, that's me. But what about you? Where is your story going to go next?

Over the course of this book, I've sought to show that there is no amount of self-help that will bring the satisfaction our hearts desire. God's grace is the answer to how we live life well. It is the best help out there.

It may be that you knew that already, in theory at least, and you want to finish this book by embracing this truth afresh.

Or maybe all of this has been pretty new to you. Perhaps you don't call yourself a Christian; or perhaps you *do*, but Jesus hasn't really been a significant feature in your life recently. If so, I want to finish by inviting you to make him part of your next chapter—to surrender your story to him.

If you are waiting to feel passionate or ready to follow Jesus, might I suggest that fervor comes not before your decision but after. God will give you the faith to trust him more, as you walk more closely with him every day, moving from striving to surrender.

Jesus offers you a personal invitation:

*Here I am! I stand at the door and knock. If anyone hears my voice and opens the door, I will come in and eat with that person, and they with me. (Revelation 3:20)*

If you want to accept this life-changing invitation, you can do so now. Share with God what's on your heart and your desire to trust Jesus. The following is a prayer you can pray:

*God, thank you for loving me and sending Jesus to find me. I confess my sins and mistakes, and I ask for your forgiveness. I believe that Jesus died for my sins and rose again, and I accept him as Lord and Savior. I surrender to your will and to Jesus' reign as King of my heart and life. Transform me by the power of your Holy Spirit, and help me to live for your glory all the days of my life. In Jesus' name I pray. Amen.*

If you prayed this prayer in faith, welcome home. I trust that the previous chapter will point you in the right direction in terms of what to do next.

To you—and to every believer who is reading this—getting to know God and grow in grace is a lifetime journey. A journey where God will be with you every step of the way. He wants you to experience his amazing grace.

I do too.

*The LORD bless you and keep you; the LORD make his face shine on you and be gracious to you; the LORD turn his face toward you and give you peace.*

*(Numbers 6:24-26)*

# ACKNOWLEDGMENTS

It feels surreal to have published this book. As I did not get here alone, I want to extend some thank-yous.

First, my deepest gratitude to my family for their unwavering support. To my parents who taught me that I am loved beyond measure. To my two brothers—for believing in me long before any book or accomplishment. To my dearest friends who inspire and encourage me in all seasons and endeavors, I am blessed to have you in my life.

To Lakeshia and Caryn—thank you for helping me get started and, importantly, keep going. To Pastor Wendy and Ministers Patricia and Taura, thank you for your prayers and guidance, and modeling what it looks like to love God and his church.

Writers need community. To Writing for Your Life, GCC DC Writer's Group, Entrusted Women, and She Speaks/Proverbs 31 Ministries—thank you for the resources, inspiration, and connections. I am grateful for every woman who has spoken into my life and urged me to commit to this calling to write.

Heartfelt thanks to The Good Book Company for taking a chance on this first-time author. Rachel, thank you for championing this book, guiding me on this journey, and helping to beautifully and skillfully shape each chapter. You have been a joy to work with.

And finally, I want to give honor and glory to God. You have been so faithful to me, even when my heart wanders or doubts. Your grace is amazing and entirely sufficient. You are greater than the world's best thing.

# ENDNOTES

1   Martha Beck, *Finding Your Own North Star: Claiming the Life You Were Meant to Live* (Harmony, 2002).

2   C.G. Jung, *Psychology and Alchemy,* Collected Works of C. G. Jung Vol. 12 (Princeton University Press, 1980), p 99.

3   John Dewey, *The Essential Dewey, Volume 2: Ethics, Logic, Psychology* (Indiana University Press, 1998), p 173.

4   "The Global Religious Landscape," Pew Research Center (2012) (https://www.pewresearch.org/religion/2012/12/18/global-religious-landscape-exec/).

5   Gary Haun, *Reflections of Helen: An Analysis of the Words and Wisdom of Helen Keller* (AuthorHouse, 2009), p 15.

6   Sonja Lyubomirsky, *The How of Happiness* (Penguin Books, 2008), p 32.

7   Matthew A. Killingsworth and Daniel T. Gilbert, "A Wandering Mind is an Unhappy Mind," *Science* Vol. 330, Issue 6006 (2010) (https://www.science.org/doi/abs/10.1126/science.1192439).

8   Nick Tucker, *12 Things God Can't Do* (The Good Book Company, 2022), p 130.

9   Brandon Burchard, *The Motivation Manifesto* (Hay

House Inc., 2014), p 135.

10    Brandon Burchard, *The Motivation Manifesto* (Hay House Inc., 2014), p 136.

11    "Olympian Jackie Joyner-Kersee, A Champion for Others," Christian Broadcasting Network, December 10, 2022 (https://www2.cbn.com/article/goals/olympian-jackie-joyner-kersee-champion-others).

12    *The Incredibles,* Pixar Animation Studios, 2004.

13    Audre Lorde, "Learning from the 60s," address, Harvard University (February, 1982) (https://www.blackpast.org/african-american-history/1982-audre-lorde-learning-60s/).

14    bell hooks, *All About Love* (Harper Perennial, 2001), p 13.

15    "How love sparks better heart health", CNN Health, February 14, 2019 (https://edition.cnn.com/2019/02/14/health/love-heart-health/index.html).

16    Marianne Williamson, *A Return to Love* (Harper One, 1996), p 13.

17    Iyanla Vanzant, *Acts Of Faith: Daily Meditations for People of Colour* (Simon & Schuster UK, 2012), p 6.

# FIND OUT MORE ABOUT...

**LIFE AS A CHRISTIAN**

*Need to Know: Your Guide to the Christian Life* by Gary Millar

**READING THE BIBLE**

*The Quiet Time Kickstart: Six Weeks to a Healthy Bible Habit* by Rachel Jones

*Read This First: A Simple Guide to Getting the Most from the Bible* by Gary Millar

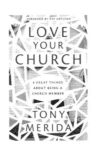

**BEING PART OF A CHURCH**

*Love Your Church: 8 Great Things About Being a Church Member* by Tony Merida

**PRAYER**

*Just Ask: The Joy of Confident, Bold, Patient, Relentless, Shameless, Dependent, Grateful, Powerful, Expectant Prayer* by J. D. Greear

*Pray Big: Learn to Pray Like an Apostle* by Alistair Begg

**thegoodbook.com | thegoodbook.co.uk
thegoodbook.com.au | thegoodbook.co.nz**